Motorcycle
Dream Garages

Lee Klancher

First published in 2009 by Motorbooks, an imprint of MBI Publishing Company, 400 First Avenue North, Suite 300, Minneapolis, MN 55401 USA

Motorbooks titles are also available at discounts in bulk quantity for industrial or sales-promotional use. For details write to Special Sales Manager at MBI Publishing Company, 400 First Avenue North, Suite 300, Minneapolis, MN 55401 USA.

To find out more about our books, visit us online at www.motorbooks.com.

Library of Congress Cataloging-in-Publication Data

Klancher, Lee, 1966-
  Motorcycle dream garages / Lee Klancher.
      p. cm.
  ISBN 978-0-7603-3550-5
1. Motorcycle workshops. 2. Garages. I. Title.
  TL444.5.K53 2009
  629.227'5--dc22
                              2009012370

On the cover: One of Roger Goldammer's stunning customs, *Goldmember*, sits in front of the show garage of an $8 million home in Kelowna, British Columbia.

On the title pages: This is Jamie's working space in Spannerland, complete with a 1949 Vincent Series B Rapide, Seely Norton Mark IV, and 1972 Husqvarna.

Editor: Kris Palmer
Design Manager: Brenda C. Canales
Designer: John Sticha
Cover designed by: Matt Simmons

Printed in China

Foreword	**6**
Introduction	**7**

PALACES   8

1 Garage Confidential   **10**
Hush-hush in Hollywood

2 The Canadian Dream   **18**
Sparing No Expense in British Columbia

3 The Presiding Patriarch of Moto Evangelism   **28**
Kelly Owen's Motorcycle Mission

4 Backstage   **36**
Jay Leno's Charismatic Collection
By Rick Schunk

THE REAL DEAL   44

5 Under the Radar   **46**
George Hood

6 Rock This Town   **56**
Sixth Street Specials in New York
By Mike Seate

7 A Fine Obsession   **68**
St. Paul's Steve Hamel
By Kris Palmer

SANCTUARIES   78

8 Heaven 'n' Hell   **80**
Mike and Nuri Wernick's Rising Wolf Garage

9 The Ghost of Villa Park   **94**
Tom White's Early Years of Motocross Museum

10 Spannerland   **106**
New Jersey Nocturnes

11 The Heart of Texas   **120**
Barry Solomon
By Rick Schunk

12 Brevity   **128**
Jeffrey Gilbert's Carefully Crafted Collection

TAKIN' CARE OF BUSINESS   136

13 Racer's Precedence   **138**
John's Cycle Center

14 The Art of Bar Napkin Design   **148**
Mark Triebold's Live-in Shop

15 Yoshi's Vintage *Valhalla*   **156**
The Garage Company

RACER'S REFUGE   164

16 Street of Dreams   **166**
Chris Cosentino's New Jersey Shop

17 The Artisan of Speed   **176**
John Hateley

Acknowledgments   **190**
Index   **191**

Let us now praise famous shops. It hadn't occurred to me before, but now I see it makes perfect sense. Men can compete in actual sanctioned races, or during envy-provoking track days, or by owning the most authentic Norton Combat twin with all its paint drips in the agreed factory-original places. But they can also compete to have the coolest, most fantastically equipped garages and shops. In such shops are projects so far beyond wicked-excellent that consciousness fails us and we become dizzy.

Most of us just cope with mechanical things using the tools and facilities we happen to have. But as we remove a ball bearing from a shaft in the Wrong Way—using chisel and hammer while looking to make sure no one is watching—we imagine a better way. The Right Way. With a special tool made for each job. In a perfect shop.

In the early 1970s, Steve Whitelock and I were cogs in the machine of Kawasaki Racing in the United States. As we struggled daily to outsmart detonation and to replace exploded crankcases before 8 a.m. practice, we sustained ourselves with Burger King—and with verbal fantasies of perfect shops. We painted word pictures of long rows of milling machines, merging into indistinctness in the fluorescent-lit distance. Each was attended by a highly trained and experienced operator in company cap, ready to render the company song while making chips fly on projects of utmost urgency. A part has failed during testing in imaginary long rows of humming dynamometer cells? Send it up to Metallurgy at once! I want three copies of their report on my desk in an hour!

Outside of our imaginations, neither of us ever built such a shop. Whitelock went on to jobs with Honda Racing in Europe, then as World Superbike tech inspector, then as AMA Supercross manager. Yours truly ended up whacking this keyboard. Yet a certain few others have kept their eyes on the Great Prize, transforming the impulses of imagination into actual creative kingdoms. Thankfully, the yearning for a personal five-axis machining center, for 140 lumens per square foot on every work surface, for every known convenience, measuring instrument, bearing puller, and exotic project lives on—yea, it thrives. Read about it here.

— *Kevin Cameron*
April 2009

Books are always journeys. You learn as you go and find new and different things as you travel along the book's path.

This book's journey started with a phone call from my old friend Zack Miller, who thought I would be a good fit for the project. Considering I've been riding since I was 11 and owned a garage bigger than my house, I think I fit this project pretty nicely.

My travels for this began with an eight-hour ride through the Cascade Mountains up to Kelowna, British Columbia, where Geby Wager, a real estate developer, motorcycle nut, and owner of an $8 million home, was kind enough to put me up. He offered up his staff to help make arrangements to shoot photographs for the book's cover with some of resident wizard Roger Goldammer's customs.

I rented a Concourse 14 for the ride and showed up for the shoot with gear stuffed into the bike's luggage. Patti Cook, who runs much of the office and promotional efforts for Wager, greeted me when I arrived. She's an efficient, no-nonsense woman who speaks her mind and runs a tight ship.

At one point she surmised that my choice of transportation was not terribly practical and may have compromised my ability to carry gear (which it had, but only a little). She gave me a somewhat disappointed look and declared, "You are just a motorcycle nut!"

Guilty as charged. I love photography and I love authoring books; but my passion for motorcycles has often led me down paths that defy conventional logic, particularly when I find a nasty little side road that looks interesting. Creating a book is much like riding those rutted two-track trails. The path can be rocky, but the discoveries you make along the way are almost always worth the journey.

This book's path taught me several things: Not only did it confirm my suspicion that my motorcycling habit occasionally overwhelms my professional interests, it also reminded me how much I really, really like fast motorcycles. More than anything, though, I was reminded how much I enjoy motorcycle people.

Many people who are attracted to motorcycles don't color inside the lines, and they certainly don't blend seamlessly into our increasingly homogenized and suburbanized McDonald's and Target world. They are people who take their own paths in life, at times in spite of cultural mores.

This makes the spaces of motorcyclists more interesting than most. They house stories that aren't necessarily what you might expect. Quite often the physical spaces defy logic from a dollars-per-square-foot sense, but they make all kinds of sense in terms of being places to pursue your passion.

All the spaces profiled in this book were created out of a passion for motorcycles, be it a passion for racing them, collecting them, or building them. The spaces range from overbuilt palaces created by our fortunate, financially successful friends, to secret hideouts, to places owned by people whose passions for riding and machines drew them to the business of motorcycles.

The spaces, bikes, and people photographed for this book are a diverse lot, all with interesting stories, and all united in their passion for two wheels. If you enjoy reading about them half as much as I enjoyed visiting them, this book's journey will be complete.

— *Lee Klancher*
March 20, 2009

Palaces

Tulsa, Oklahoma. Black gold gone bad. Tornado Alley. Dusty drive-ins and motels line Route 66, mining tourist gold from Nomads and Country Squires. Beehived belles and pomaded slicks dance the Cotton-Eyed Joe down at Cain's Ballroom.

Kids couldn't care less about roadside rest stops and fiddle players. Kids want to rip. Especially kids who grow up with gears in their blood.

Jack was one of those kids. Grew up at his dad's gas station. Took a job spinning wrenches for his cousin over at a motorcycle dealer. Drag raced the shop's Suzuki 500 twin. Got his kicks in quarter-mile hits.

Garage Confidential
Hush-hush in Hollywood

1

Jack grew up, dumped the bikes, and ditched town. Jack made the right moves. Jack met the right people. Jack went into the black. Big. The Big Black got him gearhead grift: Desmos, Daytonas, and turboprops.

I found Jack through Vinnie, a fast-talking killa from a Beverly Hills chop shop. Vinnie told me Jack's shit was sick. He had three hangars full of bikes, copters, and cars. The good stuff.

Jack was down once I got him on the horn.

The catch was silence. I had to keep my mouth shut about the location, his name, his friends, and his neighbors.

Jack heads a division for some company he doesn't talk about. Said his company doesn't want his name out there. They are on the up-and-up but run it hush-hush.

"Not a word," I promised.

He gave me an address and a time. Said to meet me at the security gate.

"You will not get into this place," he said. "Not unless I say so."

Above left: Schwartzkopf Exclusive Customs builds only custom motorcycles in a variety of styles that include stretched choppers, retro-styled Harley-Davidsons, and short tight flat track–inspired weapons. **Below left:** The silver machine on the right is an MTT Turbine Superbike, powered by a Rolls-Royce Allison 250-series gas turbine engine. Designed by Ted McIntyre of Marine Turbine Technologies, the bike is capable of 226 miles per hour and puts out 320 horsepower. Jay Leno and Sheik Ali, a royal prince in the United Arab Emirates, are two of a handful of other people who own these machines. Jack's is unique—it's the only two-seater McIntyre built. The orange ride in the foreground is the V Rex. It is based on a sketch done by Australian designer Tim Cameron. The sketch caught the eye of Christian Travert, a French engineer and former motorcycle racer who was part of the team at MTT that built the Turbine Superbike. Travert built the V Rex using the engine, transmission, and some running gear from a Harley-Davidson V-Rod. **Following spread:** Very few of these bikes are readily available stock machinery. And all of them are ready to ride.

I arrive on the dot. Jack sits behind the wheel of a big black sedan with 20s and no chrome.

He waves. I follow. We park. He opens 20-foot doors. I gawk.

Weapons line the stark space. A short-barreled Confederate—billet and sticky rubber wrapped around a V-twin. A Honda CBR1000R in Repsol colors. A carbon-slathered Ducati Desmosedici RR. A BMW HP2 adventure bike gone supermoto. All point out. Ready to fire.

The baubles sit in back with a couch and a 70-inch flat screen. A few choppers. A James. A V Rex. A Covington with a Goldammer front end. A jet-powered beast painted to mock an F-86 Sabre. A long cool blonde.

All sport tires worn to the edge. These machines are not part of a penis-enlargement program. These rigs are riders.

"I ride every Sunday," Jack says. "We have a group of twenty to thirty guys. We ride the canyons. My favorite thing to do is just get a bike out and ride with these guys."

Jack bought bikes, lots of bikes. Too many for a SoCal three-car. Needed a space that was secure and secretive. Found this place. Waited for a space to open up. Took it, filled it, and took another. Twice. The place grifts guys who prefer pricey toys and privacy. Actors. Directors. Names.

He shows me the bikes, each one touched personal. Custom paint. Hand-built suspension. A hot motor. Something. Jack doesn't ride garden-variety shit.

A couple of his bikes have been on magazine covers. He couldn't take credit because of his day gig. Says he doesn't mind, but you can tell he'd like the credo. He's too much of a bike junkie not to want a little taste.

Jack isn't missing much. He has three spaces reserved. One for bikes, one for cars, and one for his helicopter and "overflow."

The cars mimic his bikes—drivers. Hot stuff meant to be put away wet.

Jack says he owned a 100-point Shelby Mustang. A 100-point car is a time machine. The Holy Grail. It'll take you back to the day it left the plant. Factory

The backside of the garage is a place to hang with the bling. The silver chopper is another Eric Schwartzkopf machine, while the orange chopper behind it was built by Jerry Covington and uses a Roger Goldammer–designed front end.

The BMW HP2 Enduro is the lighter, faster, and more powerful sibling to the GS1200. Jack didn't care for the stock HP2 Enduro, so a friend of his made it a super motard bike.

paper tags on exhaust clamps. Overspray on the fenders. Every detail right. Judged perfect by the people who rate restos. Bona fide heavy metal jewelry. Name your price.

This 100-point Shelby seduced Jack. The guys who delivered it rolled it into his garage on a carpet. The tires never touched the pavement.

"Whatever you do," the restorer told him. "Don't drive it in the rain."

Jack couldn't stand it. He drove it. It rained. He parked it and drooled but didn't drive it again. Asked the restorer to take it back.

The restorer asked Jack if he drove it. Jack lied.

The restorer picked it up. Called a few days later.

"You drove it," he said. "In the rain."

The water droplets reduced 100-point perfection to just another 95-point pony car. Getting those five points back would take the restorer months.

"That Sunday drive taught me a lesson," Jack says. "No more hundred-point cars."

Jack tells me this, and we haven't made it halfway around the room yet. We step closer to the center. The blonde on the couch hasn't moved a muscle. Jack doesn't care, doesn't even acknowledge she exists.

He shows me the jet bike. Starts it up. The thing howls and whines and spits flame, a terrifying

300-horsepower beast of a motorcycle. The blonde doesn't blink.

We walk into the living area, and I decide to pay my respects. The blonde stares at me blankly. Cold as a corpse.

Jack tells me some friend of his made her. He says I'm not the first to mistake the mannequin for the breathing variety.

I want to photograph his place at night. I leave and come back about eight. Jack is pumped.

"I've got some new ones," he says.

I was gone for all of four hours, tops. He has new bikes? Jack knows how to live.

Triumph delivered a one-off Bonneville. A friend dropped off *Crazy Horse*, a custom built by Trevelen Rabanal for an episode of *Biker Build-Off*. The Bonnie stayed. *Crazy Horse* went back.

It's a cool bike, but Jack likes riders.

I check in a few months later. Jack says the new Vmax is rocking his world.

Also said he has a new Jesse James bike on the way, some hella strong Hayabusa with flat paint, no chrome, and 600 horsepower.

You can hear Jack smile when he talks about the 'Busa beast. The kid still likes to rip.

Above: *Crazy Horse* was built by New Zealand's Mike Tomas of the Kiwi Indian Motorcycle Company. **Right:** A painting by one of Jack's friends overlooks Euro exotica: The BMW HP2 is the German motorcycle company's sporting flagship. The Ducati Desmosedici RR is a street-going MotoGP bike with 180 horsepower at the rear wheel. Only 500 of them came to the United States, and they reportedly sold out in five hours. The Bimota Tesi 3D features hub steering, a Ducati DS1100 motor, and carbon everything. Only 29 of these were built. The Repsol-painted Honda CBR1000RR sits next to an MV Augusta F4.

Above: A BMW R1200S, an all-carbon BMW K1200R, and a battery tender line the back row. **Above right:** The bikes are real. The woman is not. **Below:** The second bay in Jack's garage holds a few of his cars. These are the drivers—a Nissan GTR, a Dodge Challenger, and a Ford Shelby GT500.

Geby Wager's garage story is a cocktail mix of Horatio Alger and Jules Vern with a twist of Forrest Gump. Wager started out in real estate when he was only 19 years old, struggling to convince his customers he had the experience and knowledge to guide them in buying a new home. He managed nicely, and has gone beyond the world of open houses and billboard sales pitches to become an elite developer creating highly sought-after homes. Horatio Alger personified.

The Jules Vern part of the yarn stems from Wager's hobby of building four-wheel-drive Jeeps that transform from a nearly normal Jeep you can pick

The Canadian Dream ②
Sparing No Expense in British Columbia

your grandmother up in to a 12-foot-tall monster truck. The trucks were built with Canadian winters in mind, and Wager and friends spent the depths of winter traversing the 20-foot drifts of the backcountry in his home-built 500-horsepower Jeep.

The box of chocolates comes from the fact that Wager is Canadian. He's unquestionably Canadian, but not in a Bob and Doug McKenzie kind of way. Unlike the typical ego-driven American Innovator that you admire from afar but can't spend three minutes listening to without the spin knocking you senseless, Wager comes off as a regular guy. He's more comfortable at a pub than a wine bar and is more likely to talk about sports or politics than discuss his accomplishments. He can make references to Greek literature without coming off as affected, and is conversant in politics, literature, and film. Credit the culturally aware portion of Wager's persona to his day

job of selling million-dollar homes. Talk with the man for a while about his garage, and Wager gives you the impression he'd rather ditch the smart act and ride his Harley or hang out with the guys playing poker.

The Kelowna dream garage personifies Wager's twist, and its three garages tip their hats to all of the motorcycle-guy garage bends. The lower garage is a working garage tucked tastefully away back by the workout room, a place to spin wrenches, disassemble carburetors, and scatter tools about. The garage under the house is parking. And the detached garage across the drive is a show piece, skinned in tin and equipped with three plasma-screen television sets, a round showroom to store your favorite piece of motoring art, and a bar and poker table for hanging out with the boys.

The garage is truly a dream palace, built as part of the showpiece home for Wager's development in

This over-the-top home in Kelowna, British Columbia, has four separate garages. Three for the guys and one for the woman of the house. The show garage has a palatial parking area for eight cars, a bar, a sitting area, a bathroom, a showroom for a motorcycle, and a small work area in the back with Moduline cabinets.

Kelowna's Upper Mission area, Woodland Hills. The area is a spine of ridge sitting on top of Kelowna that offers views of the 92-mile-long Okanagan Lake. Wager bought the top of this ridge in the 1980s, when Kelowna was a sleepy town in British Columbia. The little-known community's temperate climate made it a haven for fruit-growers, outdoor enthusiasts, and a dozen or so winemakers.

When NAFTA went through in 1988, the Canadian government began to nurture the area's wineries. With careful management and investment, the winemakers flourished, and in 1994, Mission Hill Winery won the Best Chardonnay award at a contest in London.

Kelowna quickly became Canada's premier wine-making region, winning national awards and attracting attention to the area as a travel destination and site for vacation homes. Musicians, movie stars, and NHL players bought homes, and real estate prices soared.

As the city grew, so did Wager's business, and he eventually decided to develop his land on top of the hill. He wanted to construct homes that were lavish but livable, with amazing outdoor spaces and room for the toys favored by vacation home owners.

Toys are something Wager relishes. He drives a Harley-Davidson bagger in the summer and spends his winters four-wheeling in the snow with a custom-built four-wheel-drive Jeep. He understands the gearhead in us all, and his spaces reflect that.

The dream garage house sold in August 2008 for $7.2 million, the highest price ever paid for a single-family home in Kelowna. The name of the buyer has been kept quiet, but you can bet the person is a gearhead.

The Canadian Dream lives on with Wager, and he's already designed a garage with a spinning elevator that lowers vehicles into a storage garage below.

The garage has living quarters on the second floor. The 1,000-square-foot one-bedroom apartment is nicely outfitted, with a small deck overlooking the lake.

The show garage features top-of-the-line flooring and galvanized steel walls. In-floor heat keeps things warm, and two plasma-screen televisions and a poker table are there for when the work is done.

The Kelowna dream garage personifies
Wager's twist, and its three garages tip their hats
to all of the motorcycle-guy garage bends

Left: A parking garage is tucked underneath the home with space for three cars. **Above:** The working garage is located below the show garage, with a separate entrance. This space is big enough to accommodate six cars, and has all the power you need to set up a complete shop.

The showpiece home is located in Kelowna, which is Canada's wine country. More than 100 wineries line the hills along the 92-mile-long Lake Okanagon. The lake is rumored to be home to a lake monster, Ogopogo, who is similar to the Loch Ness Monster.

The second garage is for parking, and this beast of a four-wheel-drive is a custom-built Jeep constructed by Geby Wager's company, Creative Motor Sports. The 500-horsepower machine uses an air-lift system that makes it capable of outrageous off-road behavior, yet it can also be lowered to drive on the street.

This work area features toolboxes and a work bench. The blue paint on the toolboxes is a custom color ordered to coordinate with the garage and beer fridge.

Goldmember is the creation of Roger Goldammer, who resides in Kelowna. The bike set a land-speed record at more than 160 miles per hour at Bonneville in 2007 and won the World Championship of Custom Building in 2008.

ROGER GOLDAMMER

Roger Goldammer's lean, powerful creations are an appropriate match for the Kelowna garage. Goldammer builds bikes that combine clever engineering and a clean style with legitimate performance.

Goldammer runs a custom motorcycle shop in Kelowna. He burst onto the custom motorcycle scene in 2002 when he won the custom motorcycle class at the Oakland Roadster Show with his *Dragon Bike*.

One of his most recent customs, *Goldmember*, debuted at Bonneville in the fall of 2007 and set a land-speed record at more than 160 miles per hour. The bike's sleek 1950s café racer bodywork, unpainted at the time, was later sprayed yellow.

Goldammer chose yellow paint simply because it reminded him of the old Yamaha race team paint schemes.

"I don't even really like yellow," he said with a smile. "But it seemed appropriate, and I didn't want to fixate on the color."

Goldammer *did* fixate on the design and technology of the bike—the long, low motorcycle is powered by a Harley-Davidson 960cc liquid-cooled engine with one cylinder removed and a supercharger slid in to replace it. The bike uses electronic fuel injection, nitrous injection, and a computer-controlled ignition, but you'd never know that when you look at it.

"Hiding the wires took forever," Goldammer said. "You can't believe how much work went into that."

The bike's lines are simple, with all the complexity and technology hidden underneath. The frame uses an internal suspension system, so it looks like a hard tail. The giant brake drum in the rear houses internal disc brakes.

Detail work like this distinguishes Goldammer bikes, and it's been part of why he won the World Championship of Custom Building three out of five times between 2004 and 2008.

"I pay the bills selling parts," he said. "These bikes take so much time to do right, selling them would never be a profitable business ... I do it to make bikes the way I believe they should be—fast and subtly simple."

In the 1820s, the ground under Kelly Owen's garage in the suburb of Phillips Ranch, California, was used to graze cattle for the Franciscan missionaries who ran the San Gabriel Mission.

The mission relinquished its hold on the land in 1837, and it became part of the Rancho San Jose, a private ranch worked by two wealthy Mexican landowners. After years as a working ranch, the land was purchased by Claude Osteen, a pitcher for the Dodgers between 1965 and 1973.

In the mid-1970s, the hilly acreage became a sleepy suburb filled with ranch homes and sushi joints. Owen's palatial garage stands not far from

The Presiding Patriarch of Moto Evangelism

Kelly Owen's Motorcycle Mission

3

the original San Gabriel Mission, which hosts an evangelical church, a gift shop, and a museum.

The evangelical history of this part of southern California is alive and well in Owen's garage. His zeal is for old motocross machines, and one can convert to his worldview while turning a throttle. His passion is infectious, and he's been spreading the good word about old bikes since his garage was built in the early 1990s.

Words come naturally to Owen, a man well versed in many subjects. But when he starts talking about his garage, the sentences flow like gasoline dumping into a two-stroke race engine at full howl.

Owen loves to tell stories about the neighborhood children stopping in to see his latest motorcycle

project. He restores vintage motocross racers, and enjoys putting others on the bikes he returns to their former glory.

Owen's two adult children have been putting his garage full of bikes to good use since they were young.

"A group of my son's friends come over nearly every other night," he said. "In fact, just the other night we took a 1968 Greeves out and put gas in it and lit it up and everybody got to ride it up and down the street. To see these twenty-year-old kids who ride these modern bikes get on these old bikes and ride up and down the street, it puts a smile on my face. They go apes over this stuff."

His projects are often the subject of neighborhood fascination. His garage even became a Cub Scout

Above left: When Kelly Owen found this piece of property, it was the last home for sale in a new development. He drew up a floor plan for the garage the evening after he bought the lot. **Above right:** This Greeves is Owen's latest project. The British-built Greeves motorcycles were competitive motocross bikes from the early 1960s through the early 1970s. The company went under in 1976 but resurfaced with a line of trail bikes in 2009. **Below:** Kelly Owen's 2,400-square-foot garage has one of the nicest views in Phillips Ranch, California. Tucked into the hills with Pasadena to the west and Rancho Cucamonga to the east, Phillips Ranch is a peaceful enclave of mostly ranch-style homes built in the 1970s and 1980s.

den when he invited the local troop in to earn merit badges by taking apart and reassembling a vintage motorcycle.

Owen's passion for his garage stems from his gift for working with his hands. His mechanical bent showed itself when he fixed up and sold a bunch of bicycles he received when he was eight years old. He pushed his talents further when he reached sixteen, the age his older brother had been when their grandfather gave him a new car. Owen expected the same gift for his sixteenth birthday.

"All my life, I was told by my grandfather that if I kept up my grades, I would receive a new car," Owen said. "When I finally turned sixteen, my grandfather had fallen on difficult times and the money simply wasn't there."

Rather than waste his time feeling sorry for himself, Owen decided to build his own "new" vehicle. He scraped up $800 for an old 1962 Ford van and recruited a friend to help him learn how to do body and paint work. The result of his efforts didn't match his dream after his first or even second attempt.

"It took five or six paint jobs to make it look perfect because that's how tough bodywork is," he said. "But it ended up looking pretty darn good and made the cover of *Van World* magazine.

"I just wanted to have something nice like my brother so I kept working it and working it and working it. After about two years and three hundred dollars worth of paint it was flawless."

Owen found he had a knack for restoring castoffs to pristine condition. He built a few more vehicles that attracted the attention of the local motoring press as well as his circle of friends.

Along with his mechanical work, Owen also raced motocross, turning pro when he was 15 years old. He was a very fast racer, but not quite fast enough to become one of the nation's top riders. At the time even the best professionals were living out of vans and racing mainly for beer money. Owen decided that motocross racing was not a lucrative career choice—so he built more cool cars, did some racing, and enjoyed life.

This collection of hard-to-find rubber parts makes restoring an old motocross bike a bit easier.

Above left: Owen's 1970 Penton 125 nearing completion, several months after the photo of the gas tank was taken. *Kelly Owen* **Above right:** The International Six Days Enduro (ISDE) is the oldest off-road motorcycle event sanctioned by the FIM (Fédération Internationale de Motocyclisme) and was first held in 1913. Finishing an ISDE is considered a superhuman feat. This Penton motorcycle commemorates the 1968 event held in Italy. **Below:** The shop is tidy and relatively small. Owen chooses his restoration projects carefully, and the completed bikes are not for sale.

His Penton race bike went into storage when he left for college in 1975, and afterward bikes and cars stayed in the background as Owen focused on building a business and starting a family. As both interests grew up and could care for themselves a bit, Owen turned his attention back to motor vehicles. That Penton race bike was the first motorcycle he restored.

In the late 1980s, he started doing some vintage motocross racing. He bought a motorhome and a couple of quads and took his kids out riding and racing as well. Those experiences left him longing for a better space in which to work on, store, and share the motorcycles he loved, but his property at the time couldn't accommodate a big garage.

Owen found a suitable house for sale—the last one available in a tract of 50 being developed in the area. The land once hunted on by Shoshone natives and roamed by the cattle of Mexican land barons had become extremely valuable. The house and large lot were still available because the price was sky-high.

"I made an offer that was ridiculous. I didn't think they'd take the offer. They did. I thought, 'Oh good, now I have to tell my wife,'" Owen said.

"They were really serious about getting rid of it because the economy was starting to go down. My wife loved the house and it worked out."

He drew a floor plan for the garage the same night he bought the land. About two years after his family moved in, he was able to build that garage. The original was 72 by 24 feet, and was complete in eight weeks.

His mother eyed up the big structure and immediately had plans for it.

"That'll be a nice house for me someday," she said.

"I hope you like bikes," Owen replied. "Because I'm not moving them out."

He added on another 26-by-24-foot piece and a stairway to the second floor storage area a few years later. Owen's business is general construction, and he did as much of the work on his garage as possible.

The upper floor in Owen's business office has become a museum filled with the bikes in his collection. This group includes a 1972 Monark 125, 1969 Montessa Cappra 360 (1 of 210 built), a Suzuki TM400, and a 1970 Penton Berkshire 100.

Above: Owen is into vintage tires, and the second floor of his garage is filled with one of the largest collections of vintage off-road rubber in the world. His carefully organized tire stash includes Dunlop, Trelleborg, Metzler, Bridgestone, Yokohama, Nitto, Avon, and Pirelli. **Right:** Monark built motorcycles since 1920, and the company built competitive off-road motorcycles from the mid-1950s until the company dissolved in 1977. Their machines were competitive in motocross, trials, and ISDT competition. **Below:** The photos on the walls were shot by Owen's brother, who took race photos for a number of motorcycle magazines. The bike on the left is a 1965 CZ Twin Port that is 1 of 50 in America, while the Suzuki TM250 on the right is a prototype race bike of which only seven remain.

The garage became a sanctuary for Owen. He does his restorations there, of course, and has a tidy, well-outfitted shop on one end. His bikes are some of the nicest you'll find anywhere in the country.

Owen restores only machines that he really loves, and he doesn't sell any of them.

"You won't find anyone else in the world that has a Kelly Owen restoration," Owen said. "The whole goal is not to make money. I'm trying to build a collection."

While he has a few motorcycles at his home garage, his collection is housed in the second floor of his business. He has about 40 motorcycles neatly lined up and available for public viewing. The walls are lined with photos that his brother Greg took of motocross racing in the late 1960s and early 1970s, and a few carefully chosen bits of memorabilia accompany the bikes.

"I want people to come into my museum and visualize the bikes that were on the line thirty-five years ago," Owen said. "I love it when they walk in and say, 'I broke my leg on that bike!'"

You won't find works bikes in the Owen Collection, though what he does collect is rare. He goes to great lengths to restore each motorcycle to factory condition. You can find the collection online at owencollection.com.

He loves the work and says that the garage has been more than just a place to do it. It's an educational gathering place for neighborhood kids, and it keeps him close to his family while he's doing what he loves. Owen derives some personal benefits, too.

"It is really all about having somewhere to get away from the problems in my face," Owen said. "I get a real rush out of seeing a part that was completely dilapidated come back to life. I've been that way since I was eight years old.

"As I'm working, I'm thinking about the problems of running a business. I'm trying to get the solutions to those problems, and they come when I'm restoring a part or polishing a gas tank," he said. "You are back there enjoying what you are doing, but you are thinking about daily problems."

For Owen, restoration isn't just about finding the right parts or achieving a perfect paint job on old motorcycles. He's found a place where his passions collide, and he's been able to pull his family, neighbors, and friends inside with him.

If spiritual forces still linger in these hills, they appear to be residing in harmony with Owen and his motorcycle mission.

This line of machines in Owen's museum includes an Ossa, Husqvarna, Penton, Greeves, and the Hodaka *Super Rat*.

When your fleet of two- and four-wheeled machines is approaching 200, you need an Excel spreadsheet just to track insurance and license tabs. If some of these machines require a full-blown restoration before you can enjoy them, suddenly you could find "liabilities" staring you in the face.

Jay Leno faced this situation in the mid-1990s. With his growing collection and limited time, his modest staff found it hard just to stay ahead of the maintenance. No thought was given to restoration; those projects were farmed out. But outsourcing proved to be problematic. A few of the restoration artists employed were in a totally different time zone when the

Backstage

Jay Leno's Charismatic Collection

By Rick Schunk

4

term "due date" was mentioned. Not a good situation. Somewhere along the way, Leno decided to pull all services, or as many as possible, in-house.

As luck would have it, Leno had become familiar with Bernard Juchli, a very talented Jaguar shop owner in the Bay Area. By the late 1990s Juchli was employed in Leno's "Big Dog Garage." Some of Juchli's value is derived from his contacts. His circle includes gifted machinists, paint and body men, and metal fabricators. Before long these master metal cutters and panel beaters were calling Burbank, California, home— a dream assignment if ever there was one.

For our visit with the backstage crew, we first cleared it with the Big Dog himself, who turned us over to Juchli. We sensed that acting as tour guide was a job Juchli didn't relish. Twenty minutes into our tour, we were introduced to Juchli's lovely wife,

Rosalie, who was dressed in tidy blue overalls, carrying a tray packed with auto detailing chemicals. Rosalie, to Bernard's relief, was only too happy to take on the duties of tour guide, which freed her husband to get back under the hood.

With three members of the SoCal chapter of the Antique Motorcycle Club of America—Marc Gallin, Hobo John, and Walt Riddle—in tow, Rosalie continued with the tour. We peppered her with questions, and she supplied answers to them all.

"I can detail three to five average-size cars a day," she said. "But this depends on the size of the car. I start at about nine or ten a.m. and work until six or seven p.m. Cars like the Duesenbergs can burn up a whole day.

"Jay recently drove the McLaren F1 home and got caught in the rain. He asked me, 'Rosie, can you clean

Above left: Leno has a soft spot for British machines. A Norton single, three Brough Superiors, and a lone BSA Gold Star. *Rick Schunk* **Above right:** A custom-built, steam-powered motorcycle. It looks like a mix between the Harley and Davidson boys and the Stanley brothers. Nicely done. *Rick Schunk* **Below:** Leno's Italian bike section. From right to left: MV Agusta, Ducati SD900 Darmah, and a Ducati Mike Hailwood replica. *Rick Schunk*

it up?' Of course I can! I don't just do the painted surfaces, I clean the undercarriage as well. The McLaren really took some time.

"Two very special cars in the collection that I enjoy are the 1931 Bentley and the McLaren F1. For bikes, the Vincents. But I would have to say my overall favorite car is Jay's 1956 Chrysler. Bernard's favorite vehicles are the Lamborghina Miura and the Vincent Black Shadows.

"I detail the coolest cars on the planet for the coolest guy on the planet!"

As you would assume, Rosalie and Bernard are motorheads and have over the years participated in vintage road racing on both two and four wheels. They have a matching pair of Honda 400 Four Super Sports for street riding. Rosalie has a flair for Italian machines as well. She pointed out her fire-engine red Ducati 851.

After drooling over the bikes and cars for an hour or two, our little tour moved to the restoration facility located in the second of two buildings. Here we were introduced to more of Leno's backstage staff.

Per Blixt is an expert with metal and paint. It appears that no restoration project could stump this man. A recent project that passed through his talented hands was a very rare mid-1960s Honda 600 sports car. This little two-seater had spent some of its life in the country's "rust belt," which required Blixt to fabricate many of the car's body panels. He has done several bike restorations, one a very unique steam-powered cycle. Leno loves steam.

Jim Hall's talents parallel Juchli's, as the two of them can tackle just about anything gasoline, diesel, or steam powered. Hall showed us the White Steamer Leno had just acquired.

To feed these continuing projects, Bob Sales and John Pera are employed as parts locators—a very important task. Pera's job description also includes building maintenance. He told us Leno was going "green," pointing out a large row of solar panels covering one entire roof.

Juchli said there is no average day at the Big Dog Garage.

"It seems that each day we tackle something new, something we have never done before."

He wasn't kidding. We saw a Rolls-Royce V-12 engine overhaul in progress, and work was proceeding on Leno's built-from-scratch, aluminum-bodied, turbine-powered ECOJET. Dropping back

This old soldier (a mid-1930s Harley VL) looks like it's in need of a little R&R. When an unrestored vehicle is good enough, Leno leaves it that way. Rick Schunk

100 years, the team was now also charged with getting the White Steamer running. The staff's unwritten mission is simple to state, if not execute:

Get new acquisitions running as soon as possible, and quickly fix anything that breaks.

As we strolled through the restoration shop, we were amazed at the sight of CNC milling centers, shears, brakes, sanders, an industrial-sized water jet cutter, tire changing machines, a complete paint booth, and a chassis dyno. Rosalie just smiled and said, "We've got it all, baby!" The only restoration jobs they farm out these days are plating and interiors.

In addition to collecting and enjoying amazing machinery, Leno cooks, Leno wrenches, Leno throws elaborate staff parties.

"On the weekends, Jay will take us and friends out for dinner in his 1941 American LaFrance fire truck,"

Rosalie says. "It holds ten people! When he takes a hiatus from the show, he spends all his free time here, in the shop, getting his hands dirty wrenching on the cars and bikes. And he loves to cook. His staff Christmas parties are something special. An NBC set designer is hired to decorate the shop's kitchen in a winter wonderland theme. Jay is a very kind and generous man, but he is always on! It's a mistake to try and catch him with a joke."

We had one question for Rosalie. Who cleans your car? "I take it to the car wash," was her wise reply.

Leno has a fabulous website every motorhead should visit— jaylenosgarage.com. Ride along as Jay test rides and drives machines from his collection via professionally recorded video clips. Once you visit the site you will undoubtedly bookmark it. It's that entertaining , *and* it's the closest you'll get to a visit— they don't give public tours at the Big Dog Garage.

Left: Artwork takes on a new meaning when it's 20 feet square. *Rick Schunk* **Below:** Vincents, some stock, some slightly modified, Rapides, and Shadows, all ready to ride. *Rick Schunk*

Above In the kitchen what appears to be a misplaced set of downdraft carbs is in fact a salt and pepper shaker. *Rick Schunk* **Right:** A five-cylinder (in the front wheel) Megola. No serious collection should be without one. These German machines were built from 1921 to 1925. *Rick Schunk* **Below:** Large and small prints adorn the walls. Each one is paint on canvas, not some inkjet re-creation. All were done by the very talented NBC set designers. *Rick Schunk* **Facing page:** This tidy little Triumph looks ready for a ride. Note the "parcel grid" on the tank. This was a Triumph trademark for years. *Rick Schunk*

If you need eight-valve heads for your Harley-Davidson knucklehead, the man to call is George Hood. He carefully fabricates them by hand in his garage in southern California.

You aren't going to find Hood's shop by doing a Google search, however. His business isn't listed in the phone book. There's no sign hanging on the door, nor does he place advertisements.

The only way you can find George Hood—and have the privilege of paying him for those sweet eight-valve heads—is to know the right people.

"I don't like to advertise," Hood said. "I'm under the radar."

Under the Radar
George Hood

5

That's an understatement. His business address is his home, and that isn't listed anywhere that you will find it. E-mail and cell phones are not for Hood, although he does have a 1980s vintage PC that he hasn't plugged in since the first Bush was in office.

Hood doesn't need your business, and if you aren't smart enough to find him, well, that's your problem.

Hood has a home in Orange County, in one of those neighborhoods that have been around a long time and aren't in high demand with developers. The only scrape-offs going on in this neighborhood happen on cookie sheets.

He has been in the place for more than 10 years, and the three-bedroom is home for Hood's motorcycle habit. He's got the bug in a bad way. The inside of the house is typical for a moto-bachelor,

with memorabilia, signs, and more goodies on the walls, shelves, and corners. One of the back rooms is devoted exclusively to George's other hobby, building radio-controlled scale models.

Step past the Harley-Davidson project bike sitting in the middle of the living room and take a stroll into the backyard. Here you'll find more than your typical moto-bachelor pad.

Just outside the sliding glass door is the start of Hood's outdoor shop. He has the back porch covered and filled with tool benches and a couple of lifts to work on bikes. That, and an ocean of parts—cylinder heads, transmissions, clutch plates, fenders . . . you could probably build three dozen complete Frankenstein bikes out of the piles of things in Hood's back porch.

Above left: The tank for *Geezer Rider* wears a faux *Easy Rider* paint job. Hood does most of his own painting. **Above right:** Hood's living room is a testament to the faith. The project bike in the center of the room is a real ongoing project. Hood and customer Chuck Vogel are visible through the patio door. **Below:** George Hood on *Geezer Rider*, a custom bike he calls "Henry Fonda's chopper." The bike was built from parts George found in his backyard that he said just seemed to belong together. "It's the only bike I've ridden that blurs your vision," Hood said. "It's a rough ride."

The back porch is just the start. Step through the workshop and into the backyard, and you'll find several work areas and a general, um, storage area. And a shed in back, completely filled with bikes and parts.

Hood explained that he lucked into quite a buy a few years back. A friend of his had a motorcycle shop and was going out of business. He sold Hood his considerable inventory of parts.

"I had the stuff all trucked over here," he said. "And a bunch of my friends came over to help unload it. I told them to just put the stuff wherever and I would organize it later.

"That was more than ten years ago, and I somehow haven't found the time to get it all organized."

He points toward the backyard, which is covered in Model T parts and more parts.

"You can't see them," he said. "But back in those bushes are about fifteen frames."

Step through the workshop and into the backyard, and you'll find several work areas and a general, um, storage area.

Hood points out the ape hangars on one of his bikes and tells the story of how desert racer Bob Ross invented them: He added them to his race bike so his hands wouldn't get torn up by the creosote bushes that regular handles left riders vulnerable to.

"That right there might be the bike that set the trend for high bars," he said.

Hood does have a real garage, too—that is, beyond the back porch and yard. The attached two-car is where he does his machine work. Don't expect to park anything in this space anytime soon—it's packed with equipment. There's a U-shaped walkway among the tools, but there isn't enough space to park a bicycle.

He has all the tools he needs to hand-build cylinder heads. A number of projects are going on, some of them under a calendar from 1985. One of them is a four-cylinder engine. It's an oddity in Hood's world of twins.

Hood's backyard is an outdoor shop. "This is my welding and fabrication area," Hood said. The sunscreen over the top is an old satellite dish.

"I hate four-cylinder motorcycles," Hood says. "They are miserable to work on. Most people I know who do four-cylinder engines end up nuts. I am just smart enough to avoid them."

Many of Hood's customers need parts made, and he laments the fact that much of his time is spent crafting one-off bits.

"It takes just as much time to make one as it does to make twenty," he said.

Often those customers are people restoring extremely rare bikes, looking for things you cannot find on eBay, at a swap meet, or even in Hood's backyard. Crockers fit into this bike restoration category, due to their rarity and extremely high value. Hood isn't exactly in awe of the expensive machines.

"Crockers are going for stupid money at auctions. They are not worth it," he said. "The only thing that makes one motorcycle worth more than another is three or four guys wanting it."

As long as those few guys keep wanting old bikes, there will need to be people who can build parts for rare machines, people who have mechanical talent and long-lost equipment. People like George Hood.

Once you get into the right circle of people, finding Hood is easy. Everyone who's "in" knows him. But if you can't get into that circle, forget it. He doesn't exist.

"There's a lot of guys doing this stuff," Hood says, "but we're invisible to the general public."

Left: Hood built this 1936 Harley-Davidson VLH for Chuck Vogel. The engine displaces 80 cubic inches and pushes a VL four-speed. **Below:** Vic Vogel is the uncle of the bike's owner. The paint was done to commemorate Vic's military career.

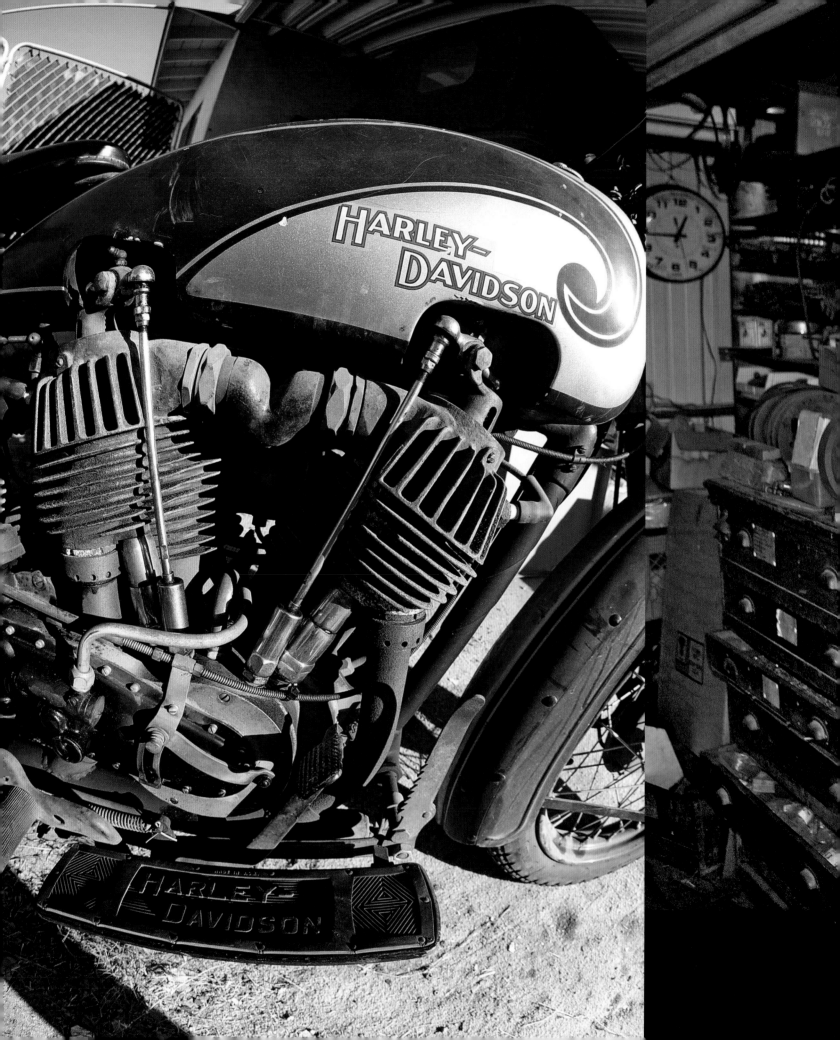

Left: Hood calls this 1925 Harley-Davidson JD "Barbie" because he and the bike tried to go through a barbwire fence together. Both carry scars from the ordeal. The JD has a stroked engine and a ratchet-top hand clutch. **Above:** Hood's place has several sheds that are completely full of vintage parts.

The two-car garage at Hood's home is the machine shop. This is the back of the shop. Parking cars is not an option.

Above left: Hood does a lot of hand fabrication at his shop, and his specialty is rebuilding and modifying Harley-Davidson JDs.
Above right and below: Hood's parts collection is extensive. He bought a collection from an old dealer, which augments the detritus of a lifetime of purchasing parts.

W hen Hugh Mackie left his native Scotland for a new life in New York City, the British motorcycle industry had just been declared dead. "In the middle 1980s, about the last thing anybody wanted was an old Triumph, Norton, or BSA," he said, his brogue still thicker than 40-weight on a cold winter morning. "People thought the Japanese bikes were faster, cooler, and more reliable, so you really didn't see too many of the old Britbikes on the roads."

Mackie, a graduate of the Glasgow Art School, was fresh from a gig building movie sets in France when he arrived in New York's gritty Lower East Side. A lifelong motorcycle fanatic, he soon found himself missing the boom and

Rock This Town

Sixth Street Specials in New York

By Mike Seate

6

rattle of the beloved British parallel-twins he'd seen zooming through the Scottish countryside in his youth. A few classified ads later, he was deluged with phone calls from riders who'd tucked away old Triumph Bonnevilles and BSA Gold Stars in garages and forgotten about them.

"There was nobody around fixing up these old bikes, and after I restored a few into running condition, riders started coming by asking if I'd build one for them," he said. "I always knew the classic British bikes had a following in New York. They just needed someone to help keep them alive."

The name Mackie chose for his shop back in 1986 proved auspicious as it developed near-legendary status among Big Apple bikers. Located in a tough immigrant neighborhood known as Alphabet City, Sixth Street Specials is part general store, part scene-maker's hangout, and part

communal garage for the city's growing crowd of retro-café racers.

In a tragically hip town where a mane of purple dreadlocks might not get you noticed, Mackie's shop has become a magnet for a visually striking crew who could have worked as extras on the 1964 cult flick *The Leather Boys*. Greased-back pompadours and black leather are de rigueur, along with pudding-basin helmets and pin-up girl tattoos. Though the reigning aesthetic is pure Mods vs. Rockers era, these guys are as eclectic as the machines they ride. Some are students and computer software designers, while Triumph Bonneville rider Mike Kramer works across town as a director at MTV.

"I use my bike for commuting around the city, which I think most of the crew here does," Kramer said. "These bikes make just enough noise to let the

Mackie started his business in the 1980s scrounging up abandoned Brit bikes in the neighborhood and turning some of them into customs like this Triumph. He's built customs for a number of well-known customers, including director Jim Jarmusch and a rental to Hugh Grant. Mackie also built a little BSA 250 for Larry Fishburne that was intended to be a present to Keanu Reeves.

kamikaze taxi drivers hear us coming, and my bike isn't exactly a concourse showpiece, so I'm OK with it living in New York."

During the early 1990s, a visit to Sixth Street Specials meant immersion in a wild, bohemian motorcycling subculture. Mackie's then partner was a mad Russian stunt rider by the name of Dimitri Turin, who loved to wow visitors by riding wheelies on an old Norton Atlas with a hollowed-out pumpkin perched atop his head. The workshop was then located in a cramped, subterranean garage beneath the turn-of-the-century brick building, and the access ramp was so steep, bikes had to be launched out onto the street at valve-floating speeds.

"It was crazy back then, for sure," Mackie said. "We'd have bikes getting stolen right out front while we were working inside, and the neighborhood was full of junkies and homeless people," he recalled with a shudder.

Since then, the vacant apartments full of squatting punk rockers have slowly been replaced by office towers and upscale condos. And instead of launching customers' bikes from the basement ramp, Mackie's mechanics now roll machines to the sidewalk via a wooden plank and a rope stretched down the stairs from the first-floor workshop. Mackie laughed when he observed that while Sixth Street Specials was once the block's bright spot, it's now the last piece of ungentrified real estate in the area.

"If anybody complains about noise now, it's because of our motorcycles," he said.

Because so many of the estimated 350 vintage Britbikes Mackie has uncovered were sacrificed to the back-alley chopper craze of the 1970s, he's had to develop an anything-goes approach to restoration. Frames are welded and gusseted for strength, and modern steering dampers are installed to cope with New York's famously uneven street surfaces.

"Any of the bells and whistles that can break when the bike is knocked over have got to go," he said.

Back in the day, a stock Triumph or BSA 650cc twin put out 50 to 55 horsepower, which was good enough to make sport of Harley-Davidson's then class-leading Sportster. But because today's street riders face a far more demanding set of conditions, Mackie has created a cottage industry performing expensive rebore jobs on the old two-valve engines, porting and gas-flowing the heads so the bikes have

Sixth Street Specials owner Hugh Mackie (left) and mechanic and customizer Fumi Matsueda hanging out in the front of the shop in New York's Lower East Side.

enough horsepower to outrun the most determined city bus. He's even perfected the odd Triton, the classic 1960s ton-up café-racer that combined a tuned Triumph motor with a sharp-handling Norton Featherbed frame. Sleek and adorned in yards of hand-pounded aluminum bodywork, the vintage street racer is good for a solid 100 miles per hour on those rare stretches of New York City pavement long enough for wide-open-throttle runs.

While the majority of riders thrapping their reverse megaphones outside Mackie's shop are American-born and too young to have experienced Great Britain's motorcycle heyday, there are a few genuine café racers parked at the oil-stained curb. James Gale rode a BSA Lightning in the U.K. as a far younger man and found himself unexpectedly reliving his youth after happening across Sixth Street Specials during a walk.

"I didn't think I'd ever see these kinds of motorbikes again, especially after moving to the States. But there she was, all battered and beautiful, and I knew I had to have her," he said of his 1968 BSA 650 Lightning.

After a careful, period-perfect restoration, Gale clocked only a few city blocks in the saddle before the bike was stolen from its curbside parking space, prompting a Five Burroughs hunt to track down his beloved machine.

"I found a young lad in a public housing project in Brooklyn riding wheelies on it and tearing across basketball courts and down stairs," he said. "I managed to get the motorcycle back, and it had suffered some considerable damage. But I'm still riding it, which proves how tough these old bikes are."

Mackie, who spends his weekends racing his vintage BSA dirt-tracker in Upstate New York, knows he must stay current and keep up with trends in order to see continued success in restoring these motorbikes.

"They were originally built to be tough bastards, bikes that you can park outside on the streets of New York in the weather and still kick right over in the morning," he said. "I've seen some get hit by taxis or garbage trucks, and the owners ride them in to have them fixed. I always tell them, 'It's still running, so maybe it doesn't need to be fixed.'"

Mackie is a racer, and most of his weekends are spent at the track.

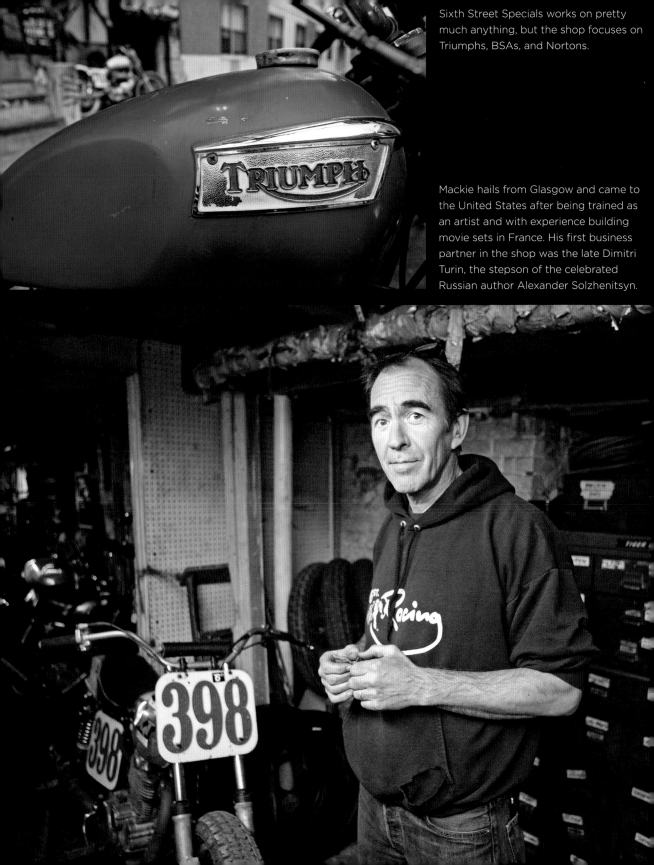

Sixth Street Specials works on pretty much anything, but the shop focuses on Triumphs, BSAs, and Nortons.

Mackie hails from Glasgow and came to the United States after being trained as an artist and with experience building movie sets in France. His first business partner in the shop was the late Dimitri Turin, the stepson of the celebrated Russian author Alexander Solzhenitsyn.

The shop is a favorite of area photographers, and fashion shoots have been done with models draped over the seats of the bikes inside. Mackie likes to wisecrack that despite the proliferation of beautiful women in the shop, the work gets done.

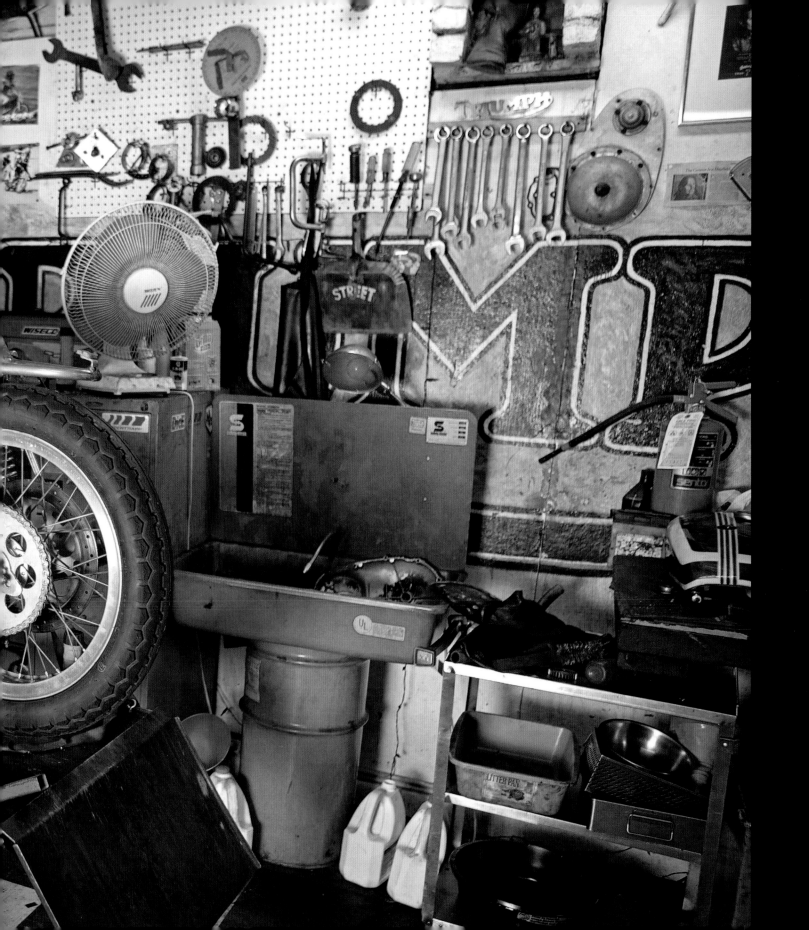

Customizer Fumihisa Matsueda was working for Hugh in the fall of 2008. He owns a customization shop in Tochigi, Japan, not far from Tokyo. His company at home specializes in SR500s. Fumi was in New York for a while, and spent his time working for Mackie

Above: The shop is a fixture in the neighborhood known as Alphabet City. When Mackie opened the shop doors in 1986, the area was so rough he had bikes stolen right off the sidewalk while he was inside the shop. **Right:** In the old days, Hugh would launch bikes down the stairs with the throttle open. The Scot has become more sophisticated in his more mature years. **Facing page:** The basement below the shop is the parts stash and home for customer bikes, spare race machines, and other goodies.

The World's Fastest Indian introduced a lot of moviegoers to a particular, thin slice of humanity determined to move fast—faster than anyone else on their vehicle type of choice—through their own courage, sweat, and ingenuity. Burt Munro wasn't just a character in a film, however—he was a real individual who set a still-standing record at the Bonneville Salt Flats. But Munro was not the only, or last, man of his type—the self-taught machinist speed-dreamer biker hell-bent on making an old two-wheeled, piston-engined conveyance move like a modern supercar.

A Fine Obsession
St. Paul's Steve Hamel
By Kris Palmer

7

Steve Hamel, Minnesota motorcycle-seller–turned-tuner, fuels his days with visions of the same intoxicating dash across that ancient level lakebed in northern Tooele County, Utah. While Munro's salt-burner of choice was a 1920 Indian Scout—modified continuously by the New Zealander over his years of record chasing—Hamel rides the venerated Vincent, likewise tweaked and tuned incessantly in search of a few more horsepower for a few more miles per hour.

Yet it wasn't Munro who inspired Hamel to tackle Bonneville's salt surface and the buffeting wind resistance that eventually stops any vehicle, no matter how powerful, from accelerating. It was a previous motorcycle speed demon named Rollie Free, who hurled a Vincent across the flats in 1948 at a top speed of 150 miles per hour. Free laid on the bike, weight over the rear wheel, in a bathing suit, maximizing traction and minimizing his body's aerodynamic drag.

"What Free did was superhuman," Hamel says. "It was comic book stuff. He immortalized Vincent." Free pushed his record to 156 miles per hour in 1950 and topped 160 for his fastest Bonneville run in 1953.

After he heard about the amazing Rollie Free, Hamel bought a Vincent in 1979. The foundation was laid, but he wouldn't set his own record for another 25 years. He ran Sterling Cycle Works for seven years, selling Triumphs, Nortons, Moto Guzzis, and Ducatis in St. Paul, Minnesota.

Above left: Vincent cam gears spread out for assessment. To the left is Hamel's Isle of Man TT record—LP record, that is. Steve and his wife, Wendy, took a motorcycle vacation to the Isle of Man, so the album is more than a gag. *PixelPete* **Above right:** The finished Vincent engine put out 95 rear-wheel horsepower and set a world speed record at 155 miles per hour at the Bonneville Salt Flats in 2006. The record he broke was previously held by Rollie Free. *PixelPete* **Below:** Hamel spent two years building his speed record bike—no easy task, but the burden is less when you have a full machine shop in your garage. In Vincent's design, the engine is a stressed member and there is no downtube at the front of the bike. *PixelPete*

"I had a lot of fun and lost a lot of money," he said with a laugh. "I closed the shop in 1986, but my customers wouldn't leave me alone."

Hamel bought property behind his old space and embarked on a postretail life, fixing bikes. His shop is an old two-car garage, which he outfitted for motorcycle repair and fabrication in 1990.

"It's been the center of my universe ever since," he says.

Hamel's projects have evolved from fixing bikes to building more specialized—and fast—machines. Most of his work involves Vincents. In 2006 he built an engine for custom bike builder Matt Hotch, who made a bike for Discovery Channel's *Biker Build-Off*. Hotch and his competitor, Roger Goldammer, ran both of the finished bikes at Bonneville.

Hamel is also building a Vincent race bike, and he's always working and learning to increase his own speed at the salt flats. He already has a national record for a modified, pushrod gas bike with no streamlining. That's an American Motorcycle Association (AMA) record, as opposed to the Bonneville Speed Week Southern California Timing Association club records, but it's still the national best at 149 miles per hour. This record class requires the rider to sit upright, feet on the pegs—which is

Left: Steve Hamel builds engines for owners far and wide—some for show, some for speed, some stock, some modified for power or to accept electric start, modern alternators, or other improvements. The bike in the back is a hot rod Vincent built to set a world speed record. *PixelPete* **Below:** Hamel's first love is Vincent motorcycles, but he works on a wide variety of machines. *PixelPete*

Right: Manufacturers have always strived for appealing badges. In decades of selling, fixing, and modifying bikes, Hamel has collected many interesting emblems, which now form motorcycle art (or tractor art, in the case of the Minneapolis-Moline sign). *PixelPete* **Below:** Building a half-century-old motorcycle to beat 150 miles per hour takes surgical care. This shot shows the engine's incorporation into the frame as a stressed member, with each cylinder attached to the upper frame, which also bolts to the original design's then-advanced mono-shock rear suspension.

As reckless as running WOT on the salt flats may seem, it's a game of extreme care and precision. The Burt Munro days of cutting down tire tread with a knife are long gone. Every part on this bike is built to handle Hamel's maximum Bonneville speed and then some. *PixelPete*

why this is a national record even though Rollie Free went faster lying down.

Conceptually, Hamel's record bike is a 1950 Vincent, but he's doubled the horsepower on that motor by tweaking it, mostly with new parts. He's making about 110 horses at the rear wheel, compared to a stock 1950 Vincent's 50/52 HP. An interesting facet of Bonneville record-setting efforts is that horsepower isn't the major challenge—tire slip is. The engine doesn't get to max out its power against wind resistance because tire slip is the weak link. Get traction, and you can flog the bike to a higher speed.

"It's counterintuitive," Hamel says, "but at Bonneville you want to be as heavy as possible." Rollie Free cheated the wind and tire slip by lying down over the back wheel of his bike.

Hamel thanks his dear, departed dad, Mel, for his motorcycle passion. "He had a '48 Harley panhead

before I was born," Hamel recounts. "As far back as I can remember, I was sitting on the gas tank in front of Dad, holding onto the gas caps on that Harley, smelling the gasoline, listening to the sound of the pipes, and feeling the wind in my face." The joy of those sensations has never left him.

"I got my first motorcycle before I got my license," Hamel said, "a 1961 Triumph Cub. It came in pieces, and it's still in pieces." It's one of the projects many others have leapfrogged over the years. The first bike that Hamel put miles on, and broke, and fixed, was a 1967 CL 160 Honda "high pipe." It's one of the few bikes he's had that he doesn't still own. He has his father's panhead, that first Cub, plus dozens of bikes by Triumph, Norton, BSA, Ducati, Velocette, and other manufacturers.

In 2006, Hamel achieved his goal of beating Rollie Free's record speed of 150.313 at the

Above: Classic machinery is the dominant feel in Hamel's shop garage. The engine in the foreground is a show motor for a custom bike builder. The one in the middle of the shot is for a hot rod Vincent. *PixelPete* **Right:** Several different exhaust pipes were tried on the world record bike. In the end, 1 $\frac{7}{8}$-inch diameter pipes gave the best performance. *PixelPete*

Bonneville Salt Flats. Now Hamel has his heart and mind set on joining the 200-mile-per-hour club. He'll add some partial streamlining, which he projects will get him up near 180, and he will eventually increase power and refine his streamlining work enough to achieve 190, which will surpass Munro's best of over 183. After he achieves that goal, Hamel plans to dedicate a year to even more development to hit the magic double-century.

A lot of learning, tire slip, and wind resistance stand between Hamel and another 50 miles per hour atop a 60-year-old motorcycle, but Hamel not only welcomes the challenge, he lives for it.

"Dad taught me basic mechanics. He was a child of the Depression. We were good at taking care of ourselves, taking care of our stuff, and not spending any money," he said. He used his father's instruction and built on it to become a self-taught machinist, fabricator, and welder.

But breaking records takes more. To hit those speeds, Hamel says you need a network of specialists and tools, or you have to acquire what you need and learn how to use it. Hamel, who loves to fend for himself and find his own way, chose the second path.

"You have to look for answers in unusual places," he said. And he's not afraid to admit what he doesn't

Pulling modern speed out of mid-century engines takes some tweaking, not least to airflow. Carbs and pipes are obvious pinch points that must be addressed on any high-performance build. This piece will flow a lot more exhaust than a stock part. *PixelPete*

know and to seek guidance from anyone who might have fresh insights.

"When I started pursuing Bonneville, I had barely scratched the surface. Now I'm scratching deep," he said. He credits mentors who have been down the path he's on and shared their skills and knowledge. He is also very grateful to his wife, Wendy, for tolerating all his time in the shop, and for taking an interest in his passion. She has a 1969 Triumph Bonneville, which Hamel built for her, and a 1945 war department BSA M20, which she learned to ride on. Not long after getting her license, she joined Hamel on her own bike for a two-week tour on the Isle of Man. Their trip coincided with the Manx Grand Prix and an English vintage rally, for a motorcycle-intensive trip.

Burt Munro and Rollie Free are heroes to the small, driven cadre who make Bonneville the center of their world. Would these legends be angry that challengers are gunning for them, seeking to knock them from the record books? Of course not, for they, more than anyone else, know the obsession that seizes men like Hamel.

Records, as they say, are made to be broken, and for many of them, Bonneville is the final arbiter. Let the fastest man—or woman—win, and inspire another generation to be faster still.

(Reprinted from *Dream Garages* by Kris Palmer, MBI Publishing 2006.)

After he heard about the amazing Rollie Free, Hamel bought a Vincent in 1979. The foundation was laid, but he wouldn't set his own record for another 25 years.

On the night dedicated to getting the bike together and running, Hamel's friends turned out in strength to help make it happen, testing the electrical system, making safety checks, and sharing all their expertise and enthusiasm. Hamel ran the completed bike up and down the alley behind the garage once or twice and that was the only testing it got before he rode it faster than 150 miles per hour at Bonneville. *PixelPete*

When a bike fires up in Rising Wolf Garage, owners Michael and Nuri Wernick play a little game. The couple works at home and lives in an apartment above their garage. They rent spaces out in the garage to New York City motorcyclists. The game is that when they hear the bike start, they try to identify the renter by the motorcycle's sound.

When they started the game, Michael and Nuri would begin with the make or engine of the bike—is it a Honda four-cylinder or a Ducati twin? The game changed over the years as their ears became more finely tuned to the machines under their care, and they now can identify their customers by the exhaust note.

Heaven 'n' Hell

Mike and Nuri Wernick's Rising Wolf Garage

8

"Nuri and I work and live upstairs in our apartment so we're always around to hear the rhythm of the garage," Michael said. "In many ways, we are the garage."

The hardcore motorcyclists and native New Yorkers purchased the garage because they ride their bikes in New York City. They met in 1983 when Michael bought a motorcycle to ride cross-country from Paragon Honda, where Nuri was the assistant general manager.

The Wernicks, like most New Yorkers, lived in an apartment and didn't have a garage. In New York, even the lucky few who live in a place with a parking garage often find that their facility doesn't permit motorcycle parking. Those that do permit parking typically forbid you from working on your bike. Parking on the street leaves your bike unprotected, and who wants to work on a motorcycle streetside in the largest city in the United States?

"To change your oil, say, you would bring down all your tools from your apartment, lay them out on the street," Michael said. "If you forget one little item or have to run to the hardware store, you would have to pack it all up, go to the hardware store or up to the apartment, and come back down.

"A half an hour oil change could turn into a three-and-a-half or four-hour ordeal."

Michael and Nuri struggled to wrench on their bikes, and knew that they were not the only ones who did. They hoped to someday open a parking garage.

When Rising Wolf was up for sale in the mid-1990s, the couple decided to take the plunge. The facility had ample space for them, and was located about 10 blocks from the fire station where Michael worked, which houses Engine 33 and Ladder 9 and is one of the oldest in New York.

When the station was built at the turn of the century, it was in the heart of a warehouse district. The historic house was designed by Ernest Flagg, an architect who brought contemporary French design to New York with his work on the Singer Building, Scribner Building, and others. The house is now a national landmark.

Michael was attracted to the house itself, and also to the East Village. The neighborhood came of age

in the 1960s and 1970s with a fantastic music and cultural scene. He loved that he was surrounded by young people and a happening scene.

Michael worked in several different houses, including Ladder Company 4, one of the busiest companies in the city. Working at that company meant he was out on calls steadily. Once he was properly seasoned, he moved to Ladder 9.

When Rising Wolf was put up for sale just down the street from his firehouse, Michael had to consider it serendipity.

The garage needed a lot of work to meet Michael and Nuri's vision. It had a mix of cars and motorcycles parked in it when they bought it. The couple chased out the cars, installed electricity, outfitted it with oil-changing equipment and air compressors, and tailor-made it into a space for motorcyclists.

Rising Wolf Garage did well in the upwardly mobile area. A long waitlist of people want to get into the garage, and Michael and Nuri don't bother to advertise. They deliberately keep a low profile, as some people have been on the waitlist for a very long time.

"This is an urban alternative for people who don't have garages," Michael said.

Success was something the couple anticipated. The camaraderie and sense of community the garage created, however, was a surprise. On a cold October day, Michael walked down the rows of machines lined up in the garage.

"Let's take this guy here," he said. "He's been here for eleven years. This guy's been here seven years. This one, he's new."

As he passed each bike, he ticked off how many years the owner had been in that particular space.

"Six, fourteen, sixteen, twelve, seven . . . so the average guy's been here many, many years. After a while, the guys become friends. It's a huge community here. We have a Christmas party every year for them. It's a fun thing for everyone."

One of the groups of friends who met there are Kenny, Jamie, John, and Jordan, who now park their passions at Spannerland, a New Jersey warehouse shared by motorcycle collectors and enthusiasts. Peter Dietrich runs a similar garage rental space, but the demand is so high that he and the Wernicks are hardly competitors.

In a city where finding a place to park and work on your motorcycle is nearly impossible, Rising Wolf Garage offers a sanctuary that combines motorcycle parking space, working space, and security.

Mike and Nuri Wernick in front of Rising Wolf Garage in New York's East Village. The couple live and work above the garage.

"[Michael] came to our Christmas party," Dietrich said. "There is plenty of business to go around."

The proximity of Rising Wolf Garage to Michael's fire station allowed some of his friends at the station to drop in from time to time. A number of them were motorcyclists, and guys who became interested in bikes often consulted with Michael and Nuri. Gerard Baptiste did just that.

Nicknamed "Biscuits" because he kept dog biscuits in his pocket in case he came upon an attractive young woman walking her dog, Baptiste stopped by one day to look at some of the bikes at Rising Wolf.

"I don't have a license. I don't have nothing," he told Michael. "I just want to learn how to ride a bike."

So Michael suggested Baptiste go out and find a small, cheap Japanese motorcycle, maybe a Honda 450 Nighthawk or a Yamaha Seca. He came back to see Michael again a few weeks later. He had found a motorcycle and wanted Michael to go with him to look at it.

Baptiste's bike of choice was a Honda CB750 LTD in regrettable condition. The motorcycle wasn't even running.

"No, this is not for you," Michael said after they left.

Baptiste was insistent, so Michael recruited his mechanic friend Yukio to have a look at it.

"You don't want this bike," Yukio said when he saw the Honda. Yukio estimated that it would cost between $1,200 and $1,400 just to get the bike running. They all went back to the firehouse, and Michael told Baptiste—again—that the Honda was not a good choice.

A few weeks later, Michael was at the firehouse and Gerard appeared half-pushing, half-dragging the ratty CB750 LTD up the street.

"Gerard," Michael said. "What part of what I told you did you not understand?"

Baptiste was attracted to the old Honda's simplicity, and he had talked the seller into letting it go for $100. He brought it to the firehouse as a project.

"Michael, you don't understand," he said. "I really want to fix that bike."

Above: The bikes housed in Rising Wolf are a diverse lot, ranging from a smattering of cruisers, plenty of sportbikes, and interesting creations like this Ducati Monster–based adventure bike. **Below:** This space under the stairs is a coveted spot as it includes a work bench. Complete restorations have been done in the compact work areas at Rising Wolf.

Left: The bike rests in front of a photo of Gerard Baptiste. When he bought it, the motorcycle was a nearly unsalvageable heap, but he wouldn't let it go. **Above:** The motorcycle was rescued from behind a pile of donations at the fire station after being written about in *Backroads* magazine. Once the restoration began, motorcycle companies tripped over themselves to offer parts and support. The finished bike is superb.

This piece of artwork was created by Kevin Duffy to commemorate the firehouse. The 10 roses are in honor of the 10 men from the station who lost their lives in the tragedy, and 343 signifies the number of New York Fire Department losses that day. The art appears on the gas tank of the Dream Bike. **Inset:** A documentary film, *Dream Bike*, was made about the restoration of the once-tired Honda. John Allison and Tim O'Grady produced and directed the film.

That was in late August of 2001. A few weeks afterward, the twin towers fell and Michael's company was one of the first to respond. Much of the group was in the north tower when it collapsed. Ten of the ladder company's firefighters didn't make it out. Gerard "Biscuits" Baptiste was one of them.

As the men from Ladder 9 picked up the pieces of their lives, the firehouse filled with donations of all kinds.

Jeff Kurtzman and Brian Rathjen from *Backroads* magazine came to the firehouse for a fundraiser in October 2001, and they spotted a wheel protruding from behind a pile of donations. They asked about the bike, but the guys at the firehouse didn't have much to say about it.

After he returned home, Kurtzman called Michael to ask about the Honda. Michael had no interest in the bike initially. "That's garbage," he said. "We are throwing that out."

Kurtzman wrote a column about the lonely bike in the firehouse. When *Backroads* magazine readers sent in a flood of letters, Rathjen decided the bike would make a good project. He called Honda and Progressive to ask for help on the project, and received positive responses.

The late Stephen Lovas, a pilot and performance engine builder who owned Cycle Service and Accessories in New Jersey, heard about the bike. He decided to oversee the restoration, and hauled it to his shop. An outpouring of help came his way as Honda sent parts and aftermarket companies supplied whatever he asked for.

Mike and Nuri Wernick on the road on the back of their Honda VFR. *Joe McNally*

The red Indian was restored at the garage, and the owner has another project bike in process.

"It was a real healing tool for a lot of people, rather than a bike," Michael said. "They wanted to have a connection with 9/11. It became like real therapy for a lot of people."

Michael retired in July 2002, after 24 years of service. He was interested in putting more of his time into his career as an architect, and his plan had been to leave after about 25 years. The additional stress put on him by the events of 9/11 hastened his departure.

"They took the bike out," Nuri said. "After we gave it to Brian, Michael and I were still healing within the firehouse and the fire department. We didn't connect to it until we heard that more was happening with the bike."

After the bike was restored, it was presented back to the firehouse. The beautifully restored machine attracted a ton of press attention and emotional reactions from nearly everyone who saw the bike.

Nuri believes that the reactions to the bike were a reflection of how deeply motorcycles permeate the firefighting community.

"A lot of firefighters ride," she said.

After the bike's initial flood of press, an old friend of Nuri's, John Allison, got back in touch with her and expressed an interest in making a documentary about the bike. John Allison and Tim O'Grady made a documentary about the bike and the ladder company called *Dream Bike*. The film consists mainly of interviews with restorer Stephen Lovas and the people in the firehouse, talking about the restoration process. *Dream Bike* was shown in a few theaters in New York and Arizona, and is now available from Amazon and other retail outlets.

The Dream Bike, in the meantime, seemed to take on a life of its own. The bike was delivered to Rising Wolf Garage, and Michael and Nuri kept it there for a long time. They would show it to people who made an effort to come see it.

Even an oil change can be a challenge for NYC riders, so Rising Wolf includes an oil change station for bike boarders.

The bike eventually needed to go to a permanent home, and Michael and Nuri decided to put it up for auction. The bike didn't meet the reserve, so they thought that a raffle would be the way to find an owner.

The raffle winner was a woman from California who bought the ticket only to make a donation and didn't want the bike. She gave it to Joe, a fireman and motorcyclist who had lost his brother in 9/11. He in turn gave the bike back to Michael and Nuri, as he wanted the bike to be in a good home.

"I know you'll do the right thing with it, Nuri," Joe said. So she took it back and worked on finding a home. After several years of making phone calls, the Hudson Firefighting Museum added it to their memorial for 9/11.

"It's such a crazy story, that bike," Michael said. "It has such a life to it."

The bike was added to the collection at the museum on September 13, 2008, and will remain

there until it moves to the building to be rebuilt on the World Trade Center site.

So the FDNY Honda has a home, and life at the Wernick's place is more or less back to normal. Rising Wolf Garage is still holding its own in a tough economy. Nuri thinks that's because motorcyclists are hanging on to their bikes as tightly as possible.

"That's the last thing you sell," she said. "Because if you get rid of it, you may not get a chance to purchase another one."

In the meantime, Rising Wolf Garage's clientele are doing as they've done for nearly two decades. When the rigors of daily life dig in and take hold, they sneak off for an evening of wrenching, bench racing, or a ride.

"It's good therapy for everyone," Nuri said. "If they need to get away from home or whatever's happening on the outside, they just come here and they are in their own little world."

Most of the resident renters at Rising Wolf have been in the garage for more than a decade. If you want a space, there is a waiting list.

Tom White's 5,500-square-foot barn is as much a tribute to Edison Dye as to the more than 100 motorcycles he has gathered for display. Dye's face peers down from the rafters, and hundreds of the photographer's images grace the walls. The famous riders and races, particularly Americans such as Gary Jones, Tony DiStefano, and Brad Lackey, were photographed and idolized at least in part because of Dye.

American motocross wasn't much to brag about in the mid-1960s. A marginalized sport at best, its leading U.S. riders were hardly able to pass the back markers racing at top levels in Europe.

The Ghost of Villa Park

Tom White's Early Years of Motocross Museum

9

Dye was born in Oskaloosa, Iowa, and later moved to southern California. He earned a degree in engineering while racing hot rods. During World War II, he ran a large engineering department and then started a trucking company afterward.

When he decided to travel Europe on a bike in 1960, the ambitious Dye funded it by launching a motorcycle touring business. His travels overseas exposed him to the best motocross riders and bikes in the world and prompted another venture—importing Husqvarna motorcycles. As that operation grew, he began flying European motocross racers over to compete in America during the off-season. That led to the formation of the Inter-Am race series, pitting the best European riders against their American peers.

The American riders were beaten soundly, but the exposure inspired racers, promoters, and entrepreneurs to develop the sport until it became hugely popular in the United States.

White, then a mechanic, was one of the young guys to benefit from Dye's actions, even if he didn't realize it at the time. He started riding and racing motocross bikes in the 1960s. Like Dye, White built upon his training and experience, launching a business that would become one of the most successful aftermarket motorcycle companies in America, White Brothers Racing.

Motocross was a passion that paid off for White, but he (and much of the rest of the industry) weren't really cognizant of Dye's contributions. That changed in 1997 at a banquet put on by Rick Doughty to

Above left: Tom White raced a 1971 Bultaco Pursang during his first year as a professional in 1972. "What an awesome slider with excellent usable power!" White said. "Thumbs up!" **Above right:** The garage has a working shop where bikes can be tuned, tweaked, and restored. **Below:** The building sits on a 3.9-acre plot in Villa Park, California. White drew the floor plan for the museum the night he bought the land. White's home sits right next door to the museum, making his morning commute little more than a stroll across the grass.

honor off-road racing legends. The guest list for the event was straight out of the AMA record book. White was particularly struck by Swedish racer Lars Larsson's story about a visit to see Dye.

Dye had violated an American Motorcyclist Association (AMA) rule by canceling a national race due to rain in 1974. That honorable action got him banned from the sport by the AMA and he disappeared from the very scene he had done so much to popularize.

When Larsson and another European racer visited Dye in their retirement, he was living in a dilapidated house. He came to the door, and when he saw two of his old racing friends, Dye broke down in tears. He hadn't had contact with anyone in racing for almost 25 years.

In 1999, White and some colleagues were talking about whom to honor at the White Brothers World Vet Championship. He remembered Larsson's story about how the influential Dye had been pushed aside. "We need to go find Edison Dye," White said.

He ran his idea past racing legend Malcolm Smith, whom Dye had recruited to ride for Husqvarna. Smith loved the idea, and he told White a number of stories about Dye. When White talked to Roger DeCoster, he had the same experience.

White went to Dye's house before the event and the photographer-promoter's daughter let him go through all of his records, including thousands of racing photos. While looking through these freeze-frames of the men and the duels that ignited his favorite sport, White had a revelation about the role his bike collection could play.

"I have the story of the early days of motocross," White said. "There's my direction—to honor the sport of motocross and Edison Dye." Dye was honored at the banquet, and he and White became friends.

The same year Dye left the scene, White started his own company. He was working for an Orange County motorcycle dealership, where he had started as mechanic and worked up to service manager by 1975. White had also designed a modification for the

This 5,500-square-foot museum in Villa Park, California, is privately owned by Tom White, one of the founders of White Brothers Racing. A 1968 Bultaco El Bandito 360, 1967 Bultaco Pursang Scrambles, and 1968 Maico MC125 are visible in this photograph. The Husqvarna on the stand in the back is a 1969 500cc Twin "Baja Invader." The bike is a one-off machine that was tested in the late 1960s, and eventually shipped to Edison Dye. He coerced Gunnar Nilsson and J. N. Roberts to ride the bike in the Baja 1000, and the pair won the 1969 race on it.

Above: The bike that ignited White's fever for vintage motocross bikes was a 1967 Greeves. He didn't own one when he was young, but he "thought the Greeves was the coolest-looking thing." **Right:** The 1962 Parilla 250cc Wildcat Scrambler is a rare machine with one of the most beautiful engines found on an off-road bike. The high-performance engine was also used in the company's road racing motorcycles. Only a few of these motorcycles were imported into the United States. **Below:** The Greeves were British-made motorcycles. Dave Bickers won European motocross championships in 1960 and 1961 on the make.

newly released Yamaha monoshock that increased the rear travel.

"That was like selling popcorn at the movies," White said. "Everybody wanted it."

White's innovation brought a ton of business to the dealership, but it didn't bring him quite the attention he was expecting. Despite the fact that White had been running the service department for six years, the owner installed cameras in his service department so he could keep an eye on his employees.

One afternoon, the owner called White into his office. "What's going on back in the service department?" he asked. "I see one of your mechanics has his sunglasses on and his earphones in, listening to music and eating his lunch at three in the afternoon."

White told him that the mechanic was eating lunch late because he had worked all morning on a client overhaul. He added, "We are working our asses off out there," and pointed out that they had 100 shocks a week coming in for rebuild with his kit.

"Well," the owner said. "We are not making that much money on them."

"He might as well have chopped off my nuts," White said. Shortly afterward, White quit and started a small motorcycle performance shop he called Tom White Cycle Specialties.

"I was porting cylinders, rebuilding crankshafts, straightening forks, and doing whatever kind of business I could get in," White said. He approached his brother, Dan, about joining forces. Initially Dan was skeptical and kept his job working for Kawasaki. As Tom's business grew, however, Dan decided to come on board. They changed the name to White Brothers Cycles and rented an 800-square-foot facility in Garden Grove.

When Yamaha introduced the TT500, the Whites had some of their sources build a pipe and a few

John Penton was an early off-road racer with vision. He approached the KTM factory in Austria in 1967 and proposed that they build a bike of his design to sell in America. They agreed, launching Penton motorcycles. The imports were very popular, and more than 25,000 Pentons were brought to America. In 1977, the Penton name was dropped in favor of the Austrian moniker KTM.

Above left: While motocross eventually would come to be dominated by American riders, the manufacture of the machines remained overseas. Gary Jones tried to change that with Ammex Motorcycles, which he created by purchasing Cooper Motorcycles and basing the company in Mexico. Only a few bikes were built before the exchange rate of the peso dropped 1,000 percent in 1976 and the company was dissolved. **Above right:** White Motors in Santa Ana, California, had bikes built by the Csepal Motor Works in Hungary. They sold a few of the 250cc Tornado Scramblers in 1966 and 1967 before ceasing production in 1968.

other parts for the bike. They went to a motorcycle show in February 1976 with a 12-page catalog and a plan to sell TT500 parts to the public.

What they found surprised them. Individuals made few purchases, but the dealers they talked to were enthusiastic about the White Brothers products.

"We sold more than two-hundred pipes to dealers that day," White said. "And we had a direction for our business."

White Brothers stayed true to that lesson throughout their history, building parts that sold primarily to dealerships. They started out focusing on suspension components and four-stroke performance parts and expanded their line to performance replacement parts for nearly any kind of recreation vehicle in the world.

White Brothers Racing expanded steadily and grew into one of the powers in the industry, with $34 million

in annual sales, 165 employees, and warehouses and manufacturing facilities around the country.

In the mid-1980s, White's interest in motorcycles did an about-face.

"I was out at Perris Raceway about 1985 or 1986 racing. A guy comes out and he's got a Greeves in the back of his truck.

"I was out there with my son Brad and we looked at that bike and said, 'Man, that's *cool.*'"

White used to race Yamaha and Bultaco flat track bikes and would see Greeves race bikes in the showroom at Westminster Sport Cycle when they bought parts.

"I thought the Greeves was the coolest-looking thing," White said.

So White and his son bought the bike—a 1965 Greeves 250 Challenger—and took it home to restore

A 1974 Maico GS400 next to a 1973 Honda CR250M Elsinore. The Honda was purchased from Greg Primm, owner of the Primm Motocross Museum.

it. They bought two more Greeves so they would have plenty of parts, but they never found time to complete the project.

Eventually Denny Berg came to work for White Brothers Racing. He restored the Greeves (work he enjoyed so much he went on to found a motorcycle restoration business).

Shortly afterward, White purchased a 1973 Wheelsmith Maico and a Rickman. More classics followed. Pretty soon, he owned a good-sized collection of machines.

In February of 1997, tragedy gave White another direction. His son Brad, a high school senior, crashed his mini bike in a parking lot. He suffered a brain injury, and lost his ability to eat, talk, see, and control his body. Nurses had to care for Brad around the clock.

"When my son got hurt, it changed our lives," Tom said. "I was told that he would have a maximum of ten years to live. I wanted to spend time. I wanted him to be able to come in here and hang out with me."

In 1999 White was approached by an investment group interested in purchasing White Brothers Racing.

"Business was going really well," White said. "But I was ready to move on." He struck a deal the following year, freeing himself to spend all the time he could with his son.

"So what does a guy who loves motorcycles do when someone gives him a pot full of gold?" White said. "Go out and buy more motorcycles."

He also found a 3.9-acre parcel of land for sale in Villa Park. The 1922 house on the property was falling down, the driveway was choked with vegetation, and a canyon ran down the middle of the plot.

The price was not what anyone would call right, but White didn't care. He bought it, and spent six years getting his museum and home built on the property.

The result is the Early Years of Motocross Museum, a 5,500-square-foot place that he uses to host events, raise money for charity, and preserve the history of motocross. The events held include

Above: Husqvarna is close to anyone who rode and raced in the 1960s and 1970s, and White has more than a dozen of them in his collection. **Facing page:** Suzuki's TM250 was developed as part of the company's fledgling motocross racing program. The twin-exhaust-port 250 was a fairly dismal motorcycle, but it is important historically. Only seven of these are known to exist. This one was restored by John Pavich.

the surprise 40th birthday party for factory Yamaha Supercross team manager Jim Perry, Kawasaki race department retirement parties, and the Desert Vipers motorcycle club meetings.

The museum is open to the public by appointment, and the rentals are used to raise money. White raised more than $30,000 in 2008 for the High Hopes Foundation, an organization dedicated to helping kids with debilitating injuries.

White is extremely active in the motorcycle community and is on the board of directors at the

motorcycle hall of fame museum. He also still rides avidly. When he does, incidentally, he prefers to ride the latest race bike rather than his vintage machines.

His museum is a place for a slice of history to be preserved, and also a place where he can hang out with his son, Brad. The building is an homage to heroes like Edison Dye as much as a playground—perhaps more the former than the latter.

"I was in the business for almost thirty years. We needed a part, we'd pick up the phone, do you have

Right: Perris Raceway is the oldest racetrack in California. The track is still going, and is owned by former racers Rick Johnson and Sebastian Tortelli.

Below: White's collection includes these two modern motocross racers. The Yamaha is a never-used 1985 YZ490 presented to Broc Glover by Yamaha after he won the 1985 500cc AMA National Motocross title, while the Kawasaki is Mike Kiedrowski's works 125, the bike that brought him to victory in the 1991 125cc AMA National Championship.

The museum includes an office, bathroom, simple kitchen, and this little guest bedroom. "When I'm in trouble at home," White jokes, "I kick out Hannah and slip in next to Jennifer."

the part, yeah, no problem, that'll be twenty-five bucks, give me the credit card number and we'll ship it out to you.

"It's not like that with vintage bikes. You may have this Ossa and you're missing the kick starter. You'll call up the guy that is The Guy and has all the Ossa parts.

"'Hey dude, I've got this '71 Ossa with a Stiletto five-speed. I need a kickstarter for it.'

'Yeah, I got five of them.'

'Great, man, how much?'

'Oh, I couldn't sell you one.'

'What do you mean you can't sell me one? You've got *five* of them.'

'Well, if I sell you one, that's one more bike I can't restore!'"

White goes on to say that negotiating to get the parts he needs often requires trading things, and it helps if he happens to know what the guy with the Ossa part really needs or wants for one of his projects. White said that people call and offer him things just to bait him, and others have parts for sale that he would like, but they simply never return his phone calls.

That kind of quirkiness is typical in the vintage motorcycle industry, but increasingly rare in the world today. White, like many motorcyclists, loves the idiosyncrasies of the characters attracted to the sport.

His building honors those hardworking, balls-to-the-wall people who made throwing roost and doing heel-clickers a semi-legitimate American pastime.

Edison Dye would be proud.

Hugh Mackie told me about the place. He said 10 guys in Jersey had this warehouse full of Nortons, Vincents, race bikes, dirt bikes, everything under the sun. A lot of crazy-ass shit you wouldn't believe. Said there were fast guys there, and some top-shelf collector. Plus an off-the-hook genius engineer who hand-built a Frankenstein Desmo-Rotax single that would powder big-bore twins into back markers.

I asked him to put me in touch with them. He said he'd get back to me, that he had to run it by some people.

I waited.

Spannerland
New Jersey Nocturnes

10

My phone rings a few weeks later and it's Hugh. He says he has a number for me, shoots me 10 digits. He says to ask for Peter. He hangs up.

I call and a generic machine answers in a disembodied voice that drones out the phone number and nothing else. I leave a message.

I wait some more.

My phone rings and it's Peter. He doesn't offer a last name, and I don't ask. He wants to know why I want in. I give him my elevator pitch. He says he might be able to hook me up if I keep the location on the DL.

"I can do that," I say. He hangs up. I wait again.

I call him a couple times to confirm, but Peter doesn't answer or return messages.

I am leaving for New York in about a week. I have an afternoon reserved to photograph the warehouse, but I have no idea where to go or when

to show. Peter might just be some Jersey jokester jerking my chain.

A few days later, I am on the phone with Michael Wernick of Rising Wolf Garage. He tells me I should photograph this warehouse in Jersey. Said the place has more tasty bits than Stevie Teez. I tell him that's funny as I am in touch with "Peter." He says that's the guy. I don't let on that all I have is 10 digits and a blind date.

Peter blows me nothing but smoke until I'm on the 10-dollar bus from D.C. bound to the Big Apple, wondering whether this warehouse thing is going to happen. My blower buzzes and it's Peter calling to say everyone but a few of his guys are in on the deal. That's good enough for me. Game on. I ask him where to meet, and he says just to call him from Sixth Street Specials when I'm ready. "We'll set it up," he says.

Above left: Vintage helmets and license plates line the wall near the paint booth. **Below left:** The white Norton in the foreground is a 1976 Norton Cosworth Challenge, one of four built by the Norton works group. The engine was developed by Keith Duckworth of Cosworth. The Challenge was raced on and off in 1975 and 1976, and this one ended up in Ian Sutherland's hands after Norton dissolved.

I shoot my brains out in garages and shops across the five burroughs, dumping cash into cabbies while frantically downloading images off my camera and onto my hard drive in the back seat. I go to Hugh's and shoot all afternoon. I finish at four and I get Peter on the horn. He tells me to take the train over to New Jersey and then the subway to his place. He gives me an address for the warehouse, makes me promise to keep it on the QT. I agree to that and ask if it's safe to walk from the subway station with expensive camera equipment on my back.

He says, yeah, it's probably OK but he isn't sure.

As I'm talking to him on the phone, a guy in denim as ripped and faded as a Bowery beat cop's mistress walks into Hugh's shop. He overhears me talking about my destination and says he's going the same way. He walks me to the train, and then gets me on the right subway. His name is Marron. Paul Marron. He tells me he's getting his modeling career up and running, and that when he came here, he felt his life was incomplete until he got himself a little British number. He buys parts from Hugh to piece together the BSA he's got stashed in his kitchen. He later sent me some photos of himself working on the bike and giving the camera the bird.

I'm late so I grab a cab from the subway to go to the warehouse. The cabbie tells me the address doesn't exist. He drives around what he thinks is the right area until I spot a guy on a motorcycle sitting on the sidewalk.

"Are you Peter?" I ask him.

"Yeah," he says. "You must be the guy."

We go upstairs on a service elevator. The hallway is dimly lit, with chips, cracks, and stains spidering paint that is 20 years away from white. Looks like the kind of place where terrible things happen in gangster movies. He opens the door and flips on the lights and all I see are motorcycles. Chest-high motorcycle stands are scattered around the room, topped with chrome curves and billet beauties. Vincents, BSAs, Triumphs, you name it. If it isn't vintage, it's race and if it's proddie, it's one-off and covered in bits. One corner is stuffed with Nortons

This conglomeration of motorcycles includes an ex-works 1973 John Player Norton Monocoque that was last raced by David Aldana in the 1974 Daytona 200. That race had an entry list that included Giacomo Agostini, Kenny Roberts, and Gene Romero. Other bikes visible in this shot include the 1974 Wood-Norton flat tracker racer (one of three built), 1970 Norton F750 Racer, Reg Pridmore's 1970 Norton production racer, a 1973 MV Augusta 750S Corsa signed by Agostini, and more.

and Triumphs all packed around a monocoque-framed race bike emblazoned with John Player decals and the number 13.

"Is that ... ?" I ask Peter, jerking my head toward the Norton.

"Oh yeah," he says. "All of Jamie's shit is real."

That box-framed piece of sex on wheels is a 1973 John Player Norton Monocoque. One of four built, and this is the beast Dave Aldana rode hard and put away dry in the Daytona 200. It's the only original one left.

Hugh was right. These cats have everything.

"Knock yourself out," Peter says. "I got some things to do."

And he leaves me to wander the room. I shoot custom-framed race bikes. I shoot adventure bikes. I shoot an RS125 in the most beautifully lit workspace I've ever seen. The Spannerland guys have a dyno room. They have a paint booth. They have CNC equipment.

The place is a motorcyclist's wet dream.

I work feverishly for several hours, not quite sure what I'm shooting but trying to get the sexiest stuff on film. It's overwhelming. You could spend days shooting there.

When I'm done, Peter walks me over to introduce me to Chris Cosentino. This is the crazy race bike–building genius everyone told me about. I expect a wild-haired hipster with horn-rimmed glasses and three days worth of BO. Instead, Cosentino is neatly trimmed with a quick smile and sharp wit. He's a chapter of his own.

Nine other guys share this space, all of them with a story. Gregor is a 2008 Hasselblad Photographer of the Year who built a custom-framed BMW with a little help from some friends. Jamie has a collection of bikes that a bishop would punch a hole in a stained glass window to own. Todd and Kenny are faster than hell, with number one plates in several classes. Jordan is part of a new clothing company, Rev-It. Andrew's an architect, and Aron's the mystery man.

Below: This green 1977 Rickman CR stuffed with a Kawasaki Z-1 motor is one of Peter's project bikes, and sits on the outskirts of his area. The door leads to the dyno room. **Facing page:** Alex Jorgensen won a Grand National race on this Ron Woods–prepared Norton on May 13, 1978. That was the last National-level flat track win for Norton.

Peter brought this crazy conglomeration of talent together. He is a semi-retired sound engineer and former owner of a recording studio who worked on projects for Sting, Kiss, and Debbie Gibson.

"I hooked up with this producer guy doing jingle work," Peter said. "We had more work than he knew what to do with. The money was just ridiculous, but it was tough. Crazy-ass deadlines and a lot of mind-numbing crap. He wanted to go out to L.A. and do film scores, so I decided not to chase that work and sold my studio."

Now Peter does some kind of machining work and builds motorcycles at Spannerland.

Peter is a motorcycle guy from way back who's been in New York forever. He rode year-round in his teens, and loved cars but didn't have room for one. He met his "need to get greasy" with motorcycles, and taught himself to ride on 90th and Columbus. Body-slammed his first bike underneath a cab while street racing. Fixed it and kept riding.

When he lived on 90th Street, he went to parties in January on his Guzzi. He had to run downstairs to start the bike every 45 minutes or it would get too cold to fire.

Riding New York led to a motorcycle guy lifestyle. He lived in storefronts and chopped holes in the floor so he could lower his bikes into the basement to work on them.

Below: The John Player Norton's box-section frame was a radical departure at the time. **Right:** Norton built four John Player Norton Specials and raced them in 1973 and 1974. This one is the only one that survived intact, and it hasn't been changed since Dave Aldana stepped off at Daytona in 1974. *Jamie Waters*

In 1994, he bought a dilapidated building on the Lower East Side. The price was right and the lower level had space to park shit-tons of bikes. He was hanging with Indian Larry at the time, and they both knew that the owner of Rising Wolf Garage was terminally ill. Indian Larry suggested to Peter that he start a parking business in his garage because all the people from Rising Wolf would need somewhere to park when the shit went bad.

Peter did just that. To his surprise, Rising Wolf was sold and continued operating after the owner died. The parking business was strong enough for both garages to thrive. That parking garage got things jumping for Peter, including his marriage. His wife rides, and it was her motorcycle that brought them together.

"I met her on the street and handed her a card for the parking garage," Peter said. "That was twelve years ago."

The crew renting the warehouse assembled just as organically.

"I knew Todd and Gregor from back in the day," Peter said. "I don't even know where I met them."

Kenny, Jamie, John, and Jordan all used to park at Rising Wolf. They met at the garage, and started talking about finding a larger space.

"I had bikes stuffed everywhere," Jamie said. "It was a real eye-opener for me to be able to consolidate."

Peter knew everyone because they'd all been around. Track days, bike nights, coffee shops—the places bike guys hang.

"The New York bike scene is kind of incestuous," Peter said.

He met Andrew through Hugh, and Chris came over to see about renting a space at his garage. That didn't work out, but they kept bumping into each other.

"We were East Village motorcyclists and just sort of knew each other," Chris said. "Then we got into racing and Peter had a dyno. No one just *had* a dyno. That's the point we were like, we have got to get to know Peter better."

When Peter found out the guys were designing and building race bikes, he offered to let them use the dyno as much as possible. He was amazed at what they were doing and wanted to be involved.

Gregor, Todd, and Chris were sharing in Union City, and they were kicked out so condos could be built about the same time Peter was tiring of his shop in Williamsburg.

"I wanted to get out of my space because it was just a horrible neighborhood," Peter said. "The

Peter's space also includes everything a motorcycle junkie could want in order to design and build custom parts.

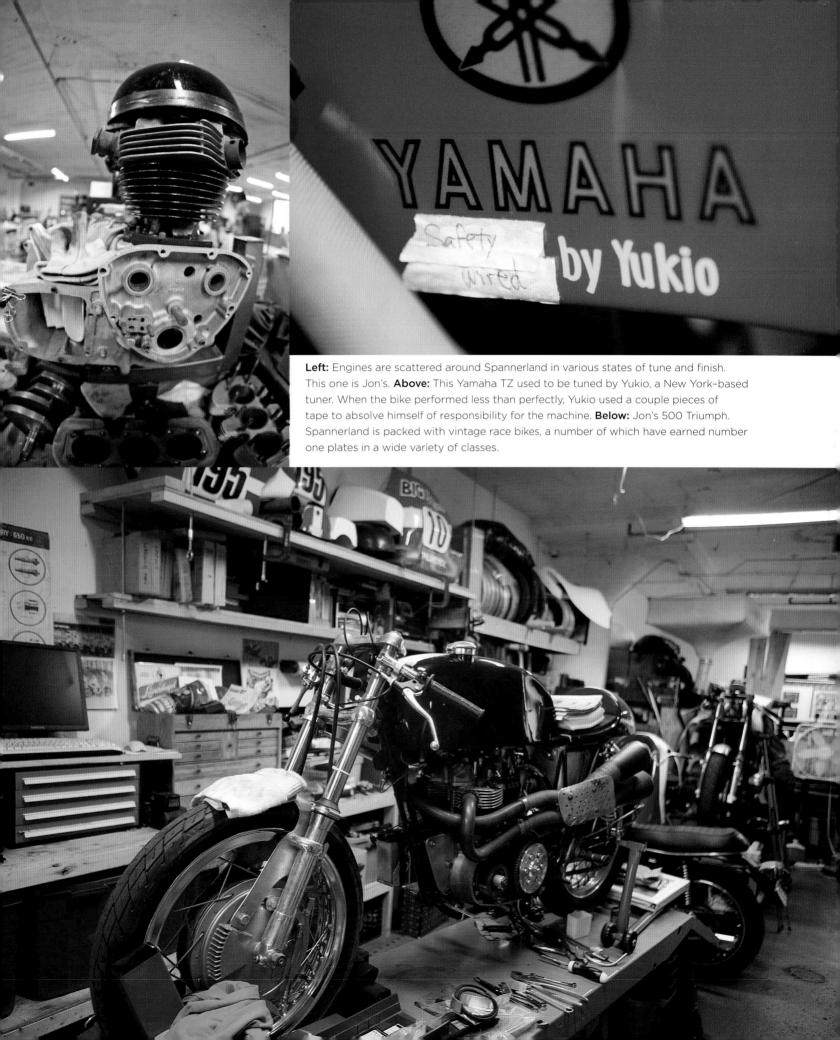

Left: Engines are scattered around Spannerland in various states of tune and finish. This one is Jon's. **Above:** This Yamaha TZ used to be tuned by Yukio, a New York–based tuner. When the bike performed less than perfectly, Yukio used a couple pieces of tape to absolve himself of responsibility for the machine. **Below:** Jon's 500 Triumph. Spannerland is packed with vintage race bikes, a number of which have earned number one plates in a wide variety of classes.

Above: The Leinie's sticker and green and white plate give away Jon's state of origin—Wisconsin. **Below:** Peter's work space has a pile of project bikes. Like Chris, Peter grew up building his toys.

building was terrible. It was cold. The floors were completely fucked up."

He and Chris threw in together and started looking. They found a warehouse that looked good, and had a 10,000-square-foot space available. They needed to gather enough guys to fill it.

"I knew that if I could get them all in on it, I could make the numbers work," Peter said.

The guys were in, and all 10 met at Gregor's studio in 2006 to sign papers. They agreed to split the costs of the rent and the construction necessary to make it work for each of them. They called the pad "Spannerland."

"I had connections in the construction industry," Peter said. "We started sheetrocking in the summer of 2006."

Peter had connections, and they all tossed in some coin. They were in by 2007, and full to the brim with bikes and projects by October 2008.

"We thought we had more space than we would ever use," Jamie said, "but even now we are tight."

They are so tight in there that a photographer can hardly shoot, and I'm spent after four frantic hours of making images. I fill every memory card I own, download a couple on the sly, and fill some more. Peter walks me out when I'm done. Chris is still working.

I walk streets that are dark with more than night as Peter roars past on a hot street-shod dirt single with flat black paint, a loud race exhaust, and battle scars.

It's getting cold, and my blower buzzes my pocket. It's Paul Marron calling to make sure I found my way back to the station. He also wants to know about Spannerland.

"Who are those guys?" he says. "Where did you go?"

I don't tell him. I can't. I have promises to keep.

Back in Spannerland, the mad wizard is building camshafts for his Ducati-Rotax hybrid engine into the wee hours. He tests the beast on the dyno sometimes late at night, the engine wailing away into the stratosphere. Listen carefully in the right semi-tough Jersey warehouse district, and the song of a desmoquatrro single might lead you to a haven for hardcores. If you manage to find the right door upon which to knock and someone happens to answer, don't expect to join in on the fun.

The guys at Spannerland are out of space.

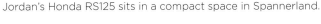
Jordan's Honda RS125 sits in a compact space in Spannerland.

Below: What motorcycle dream garage is complete without a dyno room? **Right:** Andrew is an architect, and it shows in how he's lit his Honda RS125 and the surrounding space.

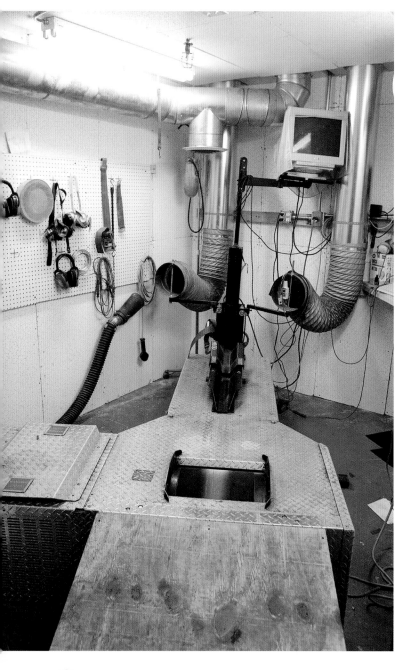

Some individuals develop a passion for two-wheeled transportation early and carry the flame throughout their life. Others, like Barry Solomon, get a taste in their youth, but for whatever reason, it doesn't *take* until much later. The delay didn't stop Solomon from assembling one of the finest motorcycle collections in the vast Lone Star State.

During the mid-1960s, Solomon's profession in dentistry dovetailed nicely with Uncle Sam's defense plans. Quicker than he could say, "Yes, sir," he was out of officer training and had volunteered for Vietnam. Instead of Southeast Asia, however, he was assigned to Fort Sam Houston, outside of San Antonio.

The Heart of Texas

Barry Solomon

By Rick Schunk

There, the Brooke Army Medical Center had a chair and a generous supply of Novocain waiting for him. To occupy his off-duty hours, he picked up a low-mileage 1964 Vespa, which provided easy transportation around the base and into neighboring San Antonio. By the time his stint in khaki was over, he had fallen in love with the area and made it his home.

Thirty-five years after parting company with his Vespa, Solomon had "a weak moment." While attending a charity auction, he watched a Harley 883 Sportster come up on the block. Since it was "for a good cause and all," Solomon found himself back in motorcycling. The Sporty didn't last long. He straddled a Harley Road King at a San Antonio dealer's open house and suddenly the 883 seemed inadequate.

Soon Solomon jumped to the vintage bike scene when a 1919 Cleveland caught his eye on eBay

Motors. "I just had to have it," he said. An even older bike then caught his fancy—a 1904 Hobart. What happened next was surely his undoing...

He visited Allen Johncock's Lone Star Motorcycle Museum. One look at that enviable iron-horse assortment made Solomon realize something about his three-car garage: It couldn't begin to shelter the bike collection taking shape in his mind. As Johncock admits, "My claim to fame [will be] that I *really* got Barry Solomon interested in old bikes."

Once his 5,000-square-foot space was complete, Solomon said "the bikes just started flooding in." He had a monkey on his back, sure, but he wasn't looking for a treatment center just yet. During the initial stages of this vintage motorcycle addiction, eBay Motors was his supplier of choice. But once he *got straight* and became savvier with vintage iron, Solomon turned to reputable enthusiasts and vintage bike dealers.

An English Raleigh, Baker, Royal Enfield, and James are mixed in with a French Peugeot. Today Peugeot's only transportation products are automobiles. *Rick Schunk*

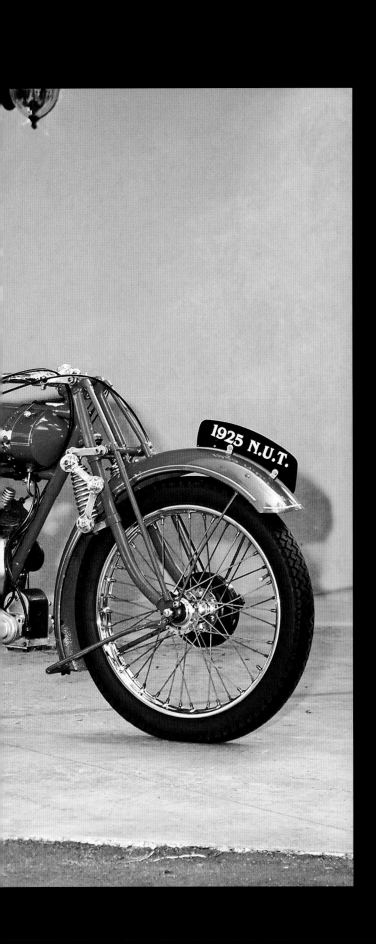

His collection tops 70 machines with just a few empty spaces awaiting occupants. In Barry's mind, they are more like art pieces than motorcycles. With his wife's approval, an immaculately restored 1926 Terrot is parked in the couple's spacious living room.

The majority of his collection is antiques. Most are from the 1920s and 1930s, but to Solomon it's all about diversity, so a sprinkling of late-model Harleys and one of Honda's engineering tours-de-force, the Rune, stand tire to tire with the classics.

Being a very gracious host, Solomon was up for the idea of pulling a few bikes out for a little sunshine, fresh air, and digital image capture. Which ones? Each was worthy, but we eventually settled on just three. A French-built 1928 Ravat; its countryman, a 1930 Gnome Rhone; and the gorgeous 1917 Douglas twin. The Douglas had recently given up its premier spot in the living room to the newest member of the collection, the 1926 Terrot.

The two French rides, the Ravat and Gnome Rhone, although not extremely rare on the world's vintage scene, are rare in the United States. Never officially imported, these two machines were purchased through a well-known European vintage bike dealer. Both are single-cylinder tank-shifters and restored to a high level.

Douglas, a prestigious British marque, produced motorcycles from 1907 to 1956. During that period, Douglas experimented briefly with different engine configurations, but is best known for its flat twins. Some experts speculate that Harley-Davidson's Sport Model of the late teens and early 1920s was influenced by the Douglas twin. Perhaps the Milwaukee firm purchased a Douglas for a little R&D. Solomon's Douglas was meticulously restored in California shortly before he purchased it. It was a treat to view and photograph these three machines in the brilliant Texas sun.

Inside the "inner sanctum," the bikes on display form a who's who of motorcycle production during the first half of the twentieth century.

The collection includes three famous makes from Italy—Ducati, Moto Guzzi, and Lambretta—as well some lesser-known Italian machines from Motom and Gilera. The French are well represented in the collection, with several machines from Terrot, the aforementioned Ravat and Gnome Rhone, a Monet Goyon, and two Peugeots.

From Mandello del Lario, Italy, a 1932 Moto Guzzi stands next to an English NUT (Newcastle Upon Tyne) from 1925. Guzzi is still in business, of course; NUT hung it up in 1933 after only 21 years. *Rick Schunk*

The Ellis Island of motorcycle collections. *Rick Schunk*

Crossing the channel, the collection is heavy on English makes. Running the gamut from Ariel, BSA, and Frances Barnett to Triumph, Kerry, Royal Enfield, and Raleigh, Solomon's collection is extensive. The sun never sets on the British motorcycling empire—and a Sun bike from Britain is among the collection.

Of course, no collector's stable would be complete without a few machines from motorcycling's fatherland. Solomon owns bikes from BMW, DKW, and NSU, as well as Rabeneick, a high-quality German brand rarely seen in America.

This breadth, joined by a Sarolea from Belgium, a Swiss Condor, Eysink from the Netherlands, and Jawa from Czechoslovakia, give the entire place an Ellis Island feel.

Two big American names, Indian and Harley-Davidson, have players in this lineup as well.

The Springfield firm fielded a 1926 Scout, while Milwaukee's old soldier, a World War II WLA in olive drab green, was seen enjoying a little R&R next to a vintage gas pump. A diminutive Whizzer, up from the minors, was also on the field.

The 883 Sportster that started all this madness is gone, but in its place are two late-model H-Ds, a 1996 Springer Bad Boy and the 2003 Road King.

And what would a collection be without a seriously irresponsible motorcycle? Solomon's bad boy of choice is a Suzuki Hayabusa.

Several scooters, both vintage and modern, numerous flags, two hand-operated gas pumps, miscellaneous motor-related memorabilia, and a high-wheeled bicycle round out the collection. The biggest problem created by Solomon's late-blooming passion for machinery is a rapidly declining amount of free garage space.

Far left: "Belt drive" in the 1920s meant (more often than not) the generator drive. This 1928 Ravat employs a belt-driven generator. *Rick Schunk* **Left:** A slippery slope, the machine that started it all, a 1919 Cleveland. Cleveland built single-cylinder two-stroke machines like Barry's 1919 model as well as a much sought-after in-line four-cylinder machine in the late 1920s. *Rick Schunk* **Below:** On the rear stand, Barry's French-built 1928 Ravat. The French at one time had more motorcycle manufacturers than any other country. *Rick Schunk*

Above: A two-stroke, British Sun, in white and green. Eventually Sun was purchased by Raleigh. The sun set on Sun in 1961. *Rick Schunk* **Right:** French, German, and English machines with a lone Suzuki Hayabusa at the far end. The Hayabusa is still the fastest production machine on the planet. *Rick Schunk*

Inside the "inner sanctum," the bikes on display form a who's who of motorcycle production during the first half of the twentieth century.

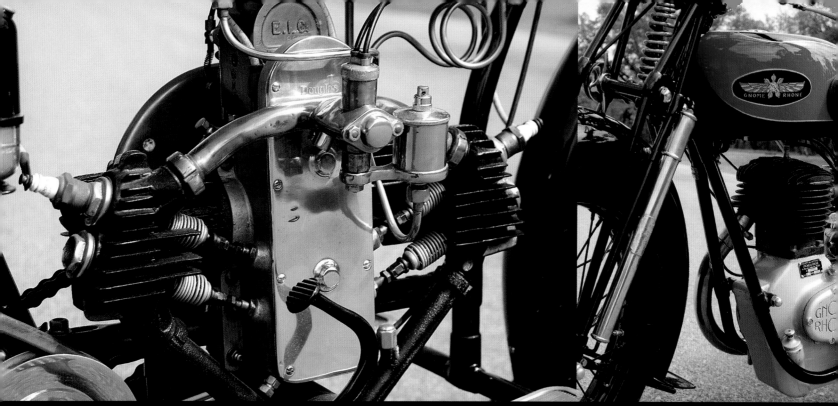

Above left: The compact, fore and aft, flat twin was a Douglas hallmark. Eventually Douglas turned the engine 90 degrees, similar to BMW's layout. *Rick Schunk* **Above right:** Gnome Rhone was an aircraft engine manufacturer before it built motorcycles. Barry's 1930 example is a knockout in red and black. Note the tire pump on the front fork—a common accessory during the period when riders were lucky to go 200 miles between blowouts. *Rick Schunk* **Below:** Douglas flat twin. The external flywheel is similar to Moto Guzzi's layout. Douglas had great success in the years leading up to and throughout the 1920s with their factory-built racers. *Rick Schunk*

Is Jeffrey Gilbert's garage a dream? Depends on what you ate before bed. For those who dream of dollar signs, Gilbert's overstuffed three-ish-car space would be worth more if you scraped it off the face of the earth with a bulldozer and stick-built a McMansion (an increasingly popular activity in the neighborhood).

Yet, valuable or not, Gilbert's garage is a marvel, with racks holding old cars and a tiny little shop nestled in a back corner interspersed with folding ladders, extension cords, and all the rest of the typical detritus of American life. A dusty black Ducati Multistrada is pretty much the only vehicle that

Brevity

Jeffrey Gilbert's Carefully Crafted Collection

can be extracted from the garage without a concerted effort.

The motorcycles sitting amongst old popcorn makers and used paintbrushes are all, well, funny-looking. One is a three-wheeled contraption up on the rack. Another was built by Fabrique Nationale, who also made weapons around the turn of the century.

Dig a little farther back in the garage, past the little gray Porsche, and you'll find some more familiar sights. A Harley flat track racer sits next to a long, lean four-cylinder Pierce, with an early Harley-Davidson twin wedged next to that. Behind them, a delicate headlamp sticks up in front of a plywood bookcase overflowing with books and yellowing magazines.

For all but the connoisseur, none of this will speak loudly. But step into Gilbert's home and you'll start to hear the music. The bathtub Guzzi in the den is not something you see every day, and hardcore

enthusiasts know they were only used as factory race bikes. The Cyclone in the dining room sounds a bell. And the Honda CR110 racer in his son's bedroom is a dead giveaway.

Gilbert is a Serious Collector.

I came to him through Yoshi at the Garage Company.

"You must see this place," he said. "Everything is … one of six, one of two, one of seven. The bikes are …"

Yoshi indicated his awe for the bikes by kissing his fingers and spreading them quickly in front of his face.

I was intrigued, so Yoshi picked up the telephone. He dialed, said hello, and handed me the receiver. Thirty seconds later, it was on.

Gilbert's motorcycle collecting roots started when he came to southern California to go to UCLA. He grew up on the East Coast, but motorcycles never entered his realm. As soon as he moved, however, the bug bit. He bought his first bike while attending college.

The 1957 version of the Moto Guzzi 500cc V-8 produced about 80 horsepower. The bike used eight Dell'Orto carburetors, and tuning the engine was a nightmare. The drum brakes and skinny tires were poorly suited to the bike's more than 170-mile-per-hour top speed.

One day while riding to school, he came across a Vincent parked at UCLA and was immediately obsessed. The passion for old bikes has lasted a lifetime.

He graduated and made a career out of accounting. It afforded Gilbert some extra income, and he started picking up cars; some of his clients were serious collectors. Yet Gilbert soon realized that he could not afford to play that game at the top level.

"Give me one hundred million dollars," he said, "and I could put together six or seven cars that would make a nice collection."

Lacking that kind of capital, Gilbert chose to focus on bikes. After collecting a group of motorcycles that came to him in the randomly impulsive ways most people build collections, he found the results unsatisfying.

He wanted to acquire a collection that was more directed, and he made The List. On it, he put what he considered to be the most desirable motorcycles on Earth. The List was based on a lifetime of reading about, discussing, and owning motorcycles. His concept was to keep his collection small and contained.

"Think about buying an art collection," Gilbert said. "Say you want Impressionists. Do you go after the Monets? Or chase the second tier and just let it accumulate?"

The List was also based on what he learned collecting cars. When he started, values of old race cars were relatively low. In the 1980s, the interests of serious collectors shifted toward cars with a competition lineage. Race cars are unique, and they often have great stories. The most valuable vehicles on Earth often have great stories.

"When the legend exceeds reality," Gilbert said, "the value goes up tremendously."

He believed the same would be true for motorcycles, and his target list included a number of rare racing motorcycles. Some of the most desirable racing machines in history are the board track racers from the 1910s and 1920s. These machines used high technology, were custom made, and competed in a dangerous sport marked by courage and calamity.

One of the rarest motorcycles on the planet is a Cyclone board track racer. Very few are known to exist, and only two race bikes are believed to have survived. The Cyclone was built by the Joerns Motor Manufacturing Company of St. Paul, Minnesota. The engine used cutting-edge technology such as overhead cams, a hemispherical combustion chamber, and recesses on the crankcase, barrels, and head to fit the engine perfectly. Shorty Tompkins auctioned off his Cyclone in July 2008 for $520,000.

In the mid-1950s, MV and Gilera had a stranglehold on world championship racing. Moto Guzzi entered the fray in 1955 with a 500cc V-8 designed to power its way to a title. The fairing covering the front wheel was known as a dustbin and was ruled illegal by the FIM in 1958. **Facing page:** The V-8 Moto Guzzi grand prix racer didn't prove to be a very successful machine. Overly complex and fragile, the high horsepower engine wasn't enough to overcome the machine's poor handling and reliability. This 1957 Moto Guzzi V-8 Mark III is the last of that breed and is one of the rarest factory racers that exist today.

The races began on velodromes and eventually moved to larger facilities designed to permit two motorcycles to race side-by-side at speeds that exceeded 110 miles per hour. Spectators watched the races from grandstands above the track, meaning that if the bikes crashed, they flew into the stands. Not surprisingly, board track racing fell out of favor after several highly publicized crashes that killed riders and fans.

The exotic, limited-production motorcycles built for the races are now rare and extremely valuable. The Cyclones were one of the fastest board track racers in the early 1910s. Fewer than a dozen of the twin-cylinder machines survive today, and only two of those are race bikes.

When Gilbert made his list, a Cyclone racer was one of the bikes near the top of it. He first heard of

one selling at a Harrah's auction in the early 1980s. He began seriously seeking one out after that.

"There was one Cyclone in Oakland in a collection owned by a bad guy who went to prison," Gilbert said. The bike was being brokered by Daniel Statnekov. Gilbert tried to purchase the bike, but Statnekov ultimately purchased the Cyclone. He also accumulated a large collection of significant Harley-Davidson racing motorcycles, seven of which were sold to the Motor Company for a sum rumored to be about $3 million.

Gilbert found another Cyclone for sale in an ad in *Cycle News*. The ad was taken out by the man who purchased the Cyclone at the Harrah's auction. As soon as Gilbert could get the man on the phone, he made arrangements to purchase the bike. It was in pieces, but Gilbert didn't care. He had it meticulously

restored by Mike Parti, and the extremely rare machine was featured in the Guggenheim Museum show "The Art of the Motorcycle."

"That's the most important bike in the collection, at least in measure of value," Gilbert said. "And how else are you going to measure?"

By that measure, the Cyclone could very well be the most important bike in the world, as very few would be valued as highly.

Gilbert continued to acquire machines on his list. He admits that The List was not perfectly hard and fast, but rather something that grew and changed a bit as he acquired.

"Everything is organic and has elements of serendipity in it," he said.

In the end, The List is personal. It doesn't include any hill-climbers because Gilbert doesn't like them, and nothing is later than 1970. He takes great pride in the brevity of his list, and believes that too many people measure motorcycle collectors by quantity rather than quality.

The question is not how many but how significant. His collection has some of the most significant bikes in history, and many of them are racers with stories.

To his wife, however, they all are invaders into the territory she has staked out in their home. Gilbert's

bikes don't run, nor do they even contain fluids, both measures taken for the sake of preservation. If the bikes never have fluids, they won't degrade. And if they don't leak oil on the living room floor, Gilbert's life expectancy increases as well.

Gilbert acknowledges that The List can never be perfect and is a reflection of his own idiosyncratic tastes.

"There are and constantly will be mistakes," Gilbert said of his list. "It's not a perfect world."

The validity of The List can and will be debated by historians, collectors, and bench racers. I do not wish to enter that arena, nor would I pretend to have the knowledge or authority to do so.

The value of The List in my eyes is sociological rather than historical. The List contains 28 great stories embodied in motorcycles. Gilbert's brief collection is getting big. He acknowledges that space is one of the constraints he faces as he collects—the amount available in his California home is not large.

Despite the fact that more bikes will probably mean fewer pieces of household furniture, I hope Gilbert's verbose tendencies continue both in life and in his passion for collecting motorcycles.

Gilbert's garage is packed with some of the rarest motorcycles on Earth, and few collectors would kick out one of his cars, either. The authentic Cobra is signed by Carroll Shelby on the glove box door.

Above left: A 1941 Crocker is on Gilbert's list and in his collection. Company founder Al Crocker built motorcycles with looks that matched their performance. The machines came from the factory with a guarantee: if any of them are beat by a stock Harley-Davidson or Indian, the full purchase price would be refunded. No one cashed in. Fewer than 100 Crockers were built. **Above right:** The Vincent Lightning is one of the most iconic motorcycles on the planet. Introduced in 1948 as a limited-production high-performance version of the Vincent Black Shadow, it is believed that only 31 Lightnings were built. The hand-assembled-and-fitted engines produced 70 horsepower, and the bikes were capable of 150 miles per hour. Rollie Free set a world land speed record of 150.313 miles per hour on a Vincent Lightning. He did so stretched out on the bike and wearing nothing but a speedo and a helmet. The photograph of Free blasting down the salt flats is perhaps the best-known image in motorcycling.

THE LIST

This is Gilbert's collection of machines, methodically built from a list of his favorite motorcycles of all time. While you can argue about what is missing, you cannot argue that Gilbert's collection is one of the most significant in existence today.

1885 Daimler Reitwagen (Replica)	1935 Indian DT 15
1899 Rochet Quadra-Cycle	1941 Indian Four
1909 Harley-Davidson Model 5	1941 Indian DT 41
1911 Harley-Davidson Model 7	1941 Crocker
1912 Harley-Davidson Model X8BE	1954 CZ 350 Factory Racer
1912 Pierce Four-cylinder	1955 Vincent Lightning
1913 Pierce Model 13-B	1957 Moto Guzzi V-8 Mark III
1914 Fabrique Nationale Single	1960 Honda RC161
1914 Cyclone Racer	1962 Matchless G50
1919 Indian Four-valve	1962 Honda CR110
1920 Indian Daytona/W/Flxi	1963 Norton Manx 30M
1923 Ace Four-cylinder Sport/Xp4	1966 Triumph TT120
1924 Harley-Davidson Eight-valve	1968 Harley-Davidson KRTT

At John's Cycle Center, the pop is in a sticker-coated glass-doored cooler and the pretzels sit out on the counter in one of those giant containers you can find at Sam's Club for 10 bucks. The parts in stock range from battery tenders and Drag Specialties goodies for your Sporty to 1960s Triumph twin rocker boxes and one-off factory race cams.

The pop is a buck, the pretzels are free, and the parts are for sale only to the right people.

Robert Genise has a treasure trove of vintage speed parts in his shop. But if you don't plan to thrash them, don't ask to buy.

Racer's Precedence 13
John's Cycle Center

"You need cases," Genise said. "If you are another shop, I'd rather not sell it. If you are racing, you and I can work with each other."

Genise has a soft spot for racers. He spent much of his life at the track, racing in the days when you could morph a flat tracker to a roadracer to a TT bike by changing the tires. The motorcycles he rode, sold, and loved were not museum pieces. They were purpose-built, duct-taped, and asphalt-spattered tools designed to win.

He and his two brothers—Frankie and John—started John's Cycle Center in the 1950s. They were racers, and they wanted to meld their passion with their livelihood. The shop made just enough money to keep the guys in gas and beer money. Their weekends were spent packed into a van and traveling to the races with their buddies.

"We would go racing on a Friday night. It would be the three of us in the van. It was comical, all of us

would throw a couple of dollars on the engine cover. 'We're going racing!'"

The guys—John, Robert, Frankie, the Greek, and more—would spend a week on the road. They'd pile into one hotel room to save money and would hit four or five different races. Scrambles, TT, roadracing, and flat track were all open to them, and they'd spend the weekend on the road at tracks like Laconia and Loudon.

The shop would simply be closed up with a sign in the window: "Gone racing."

The scene at the tracks was loose, wild, and fun. One of the tracks Genise remembers had a bar right in the middle where all the racers would meet afterward. Fans would gather and bet on the races. Gary Nixon would do wheelies on the track, and the track owners would pass a hat to collect some cash and keep the place open.

"That was the wildest place you would ever want to go," Genise said. "You'll never see that again."

John's Cycle Center is located in Woodside, New York, not far off of Queens Boulevard. The business has been in existence since the mid-1950s and in the present location since 1970.

The racers from that era were a different breed—guys who could wrench on their own bikes, who raced for gas money and beer.

"That's when, sad to say, men were men," Genise said. "They went out, they had trouble, they fixed their bike, they raced. That was it. They drove there. They would drive all around the world just to go racing."

In the 1960s and 1970s, John's Cycle Center sold a lot of new bikes. BSAs and Triumphs were in demand in those days, and buyers were clamoring. The tiny shop stocked one of each of the new models, and Genise would make a run once or twice a week to pick up bikes.

"Every week, I would make a run to Baltimore," Genise said. "I would pick up seven on Monday and by Wednesday they would be gone. Friday there was more to pick up."

That good business simply meant that the brothers had more money for racing. Expansion was an option, but it wasn't the route for these guys. They simply wanted to live the motorcycle life. A mega-dealership was not in their future.

Right: The mix of bikes on the floor range from 1965 BMWs to 1980 Sportsters. The shop takes bikes dealerships won't touch. And locals can't touch their own bikes if they live in an apartment. "Around here, if you rent a garage, you only park your bike," Robert Genise said. "You don't even change a light bulb. If you change a light bulb, they throw you out. If your friends come over to meet you and hang out near the bike, they throw you out." **Below:** While other shops expanded to become motorcycle malls, John's Cycle Center stuck to its modest location. The owner is as busy as he wants to be.

That racing history earned them the right to get a ton of race parts coming into the shop. Triumph and BSA would send over bits that have ended up stashed in the small space, which is crowded with race pipes, frames, and all kinds of goodies.

Genise has no interest in selling these parts to the collectors, speculators, and restoration addicts building bikes to be displayed, shown, or sold for a profit. If you are building a bike to take to the track, however, he'll talk to you.

"Hugh at Sixth Street, he's the same thing," Genise said. "He's a dinosaur like me. He still favors the old-time racing. I helped him out with a couple of things, too."

Hugh Mackie was building a race bike, and heard that Genise had a few parts. So he stopped in to see what might be resting in the shop.

"I got a set of cans," Genise said. "I don't know where I put 'em, but I got 'em. I says, 'you know what, I got a frame also'. It was brand-new.

"I know he's going to put it use."

As Genise thought and looked around, he remembered more parts he had. He found a factory race head. He found rocker boxes. He offered all of this unobtainium up to the cause.

"You can have that for racing," he told Mackie, "but you can't sell it."

That wasn't a problem for Mackie, a man whose personal bikes are used and abused whether they live on the track or the boulevards.

So the treasure trove of history tucked away into John's Cycle Center is not available to just anyone. The place is an anachronism, and many of John's customers bring bikes that no one else understands or is willing to touch. A good percentage of the bikes are Triumphs and BSAs—those that he and his brothers spent years racing and riding. But he also takes in old Japanese bikes and plenty of older Harley-Davidsons.

The shop and the man are both time warps. John's has no finance department, jewelry counter, or even a service department. The entire space is

The business done at John's takes place at this counter. "People call up and say, 'What's your fax?' I don't have a fax. 'What's your cell?' I don't have that either!" Genise said. What he does have is an eclectic collection of vintage speed parts and service for any bike under the sun. "I got a thing towards racers," he said. "I was a racer myself. For them, yeah, I can help you. Anyone else, it's not for sale."

LABOR
RATE
$70.00
PER HOUR
MIN. CHARGE
$50.00

LABOR RATES
• MECHANICAL $70.00
• ELECTRICAL $80.00
• DIAGNOSTIC $90.00

LABOR RATES ARE COMPUTED BY CLOCK
HOURS AND/OR FLAT RATE MANUAL

NOTICE
AN ADDITIONAL CHARGE
WILL BE MADE FOR
INSTALLATION OF PARTS
PURCHASED ELSEWHERE
WITH NO GUARANTEE
ON THOSE PARTS

ALL REPAIRS
CASH
OR YOUR
CREDIT CARD

ALL VEHICLES
MUST BE PICKED UP WITHIN
5 DAYS AFTER NOTIFICATION
COMPLETION OF REPAIRS.
OTHERWISE A CHARGE OF
$5.00 PER DAY WILL BE MADE
FOR STORAGE.

NO SMOKING

Left: The parts collection at John's is a treasure trove of vintage goodies, bits that have found a home in the shop during its more than four decades of life. **Above:** The wall signs haven't changed much through the years. In the shop's racing heyday, they would put a sign up in the window that said, "Gone Racing," and lock the place up for a week. **Below:** Owner Robert Genise works the counter with a couple of regulars, Louis Chandez (left) and Hoss. These guys have been coming to John's to talk motorcycles since the 1960s.

smaller than the typical bathroom in a new Harley-Davidson shop. Genise doesn't have a website or even a fax machine. He responds tartly when I ask if he has an e-mail address.

"What, are you kidding?" he said. "I still have a rotary phone."

Like most small business owners, he works harder and longer than most regular folk. But he loves the work, and the rhythms of his day are his own.

"I own the building, I own the property, and I own the business," he said. "If I don't want to work that day, I sit down and do absolutely nothing."

Genise is the last of the three brothers still in this business. He was 63 years old in October 2008, and considers the work more retirement than a job. John passed away and Frankie is down in Florida living the good life.

John's Cycle Center is regularly frequented by the old wrecking crew, guys who come by to hang out with an old friend. If you are looking to score some parts for a concours restoration or put your crotch rocket on the dyno, John's is probably not the best choice. But if your bike leaks a little oil and has seen better days, head over to Queens.

And if your idea of a good time with your old bike includes taking it out for a run at the drag strip, on a road course, or anywhere else where throttles get turned in anger, Genise will be happy to help you keep the wick turned up.

They simply wanted to live the motorcycle life. A mega-dealership was not in their future.

The yellow and white Yamaha 500 single flat tracker came to the shop as a box of parts. The owner started to restore the bike and gave up. He dropped it off and told Robert to do what he could when he had time. Genise has it 90 percent together. "He was here the other day," Genise said. "He told me, 'Wow, I didn't think you'd even get it that far!'"

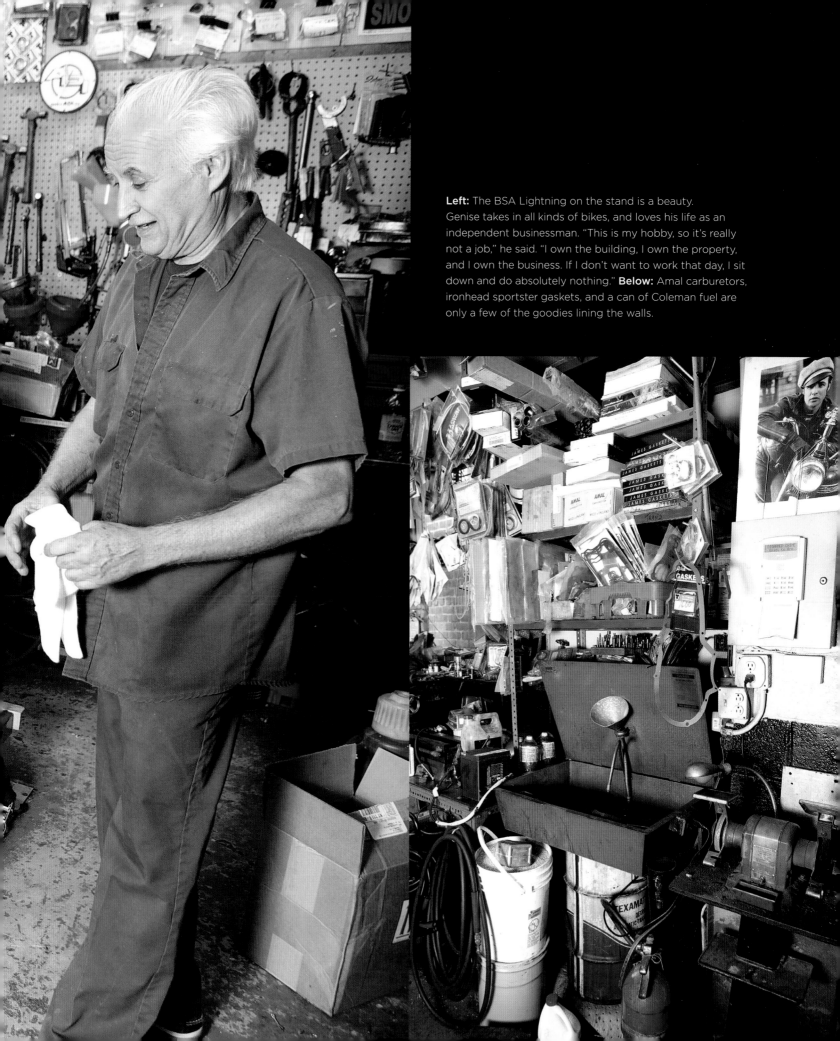

Left: The BSA Lightning on the stand is a beauty. Genise takes in all kinds of bikes, and loves his life as an independent businessman. "This is my hobby, so it's really not a job," he said. "I own the building, I own the property, and I own the business. If I don't want to work that day, I sit down and do absolutely nothing." **Below:** Amal carburetors, ironhead sportster gaskets, and a can of Coleman fuel are only a few of the goodies lining the walls.

Herb Kelleher, the founder of Southwest Airlines, supposedly drew his plan for the airline on a cocktail napkin during a night on the town in San Antonio. Sketches on this medium led a friend of mine to build a shark cage at 3 a.m. in a landlocked state. For better or worse, bar napkins are catalysts. Mark Triebold's garage, shop, and home in Somerset, Wisconsin, is just such a creation.

"A lot of it kind of built itself," he said with a laugh. "It was pretty rough on paper. It was essentially done from bar napkin sketches. I'd take the bar napkin sketches and transfer them to some kind of grid paper. Rooms will be this size and lay here. The drawings were very simple.

The Art of Bar Napkin Design
Mark Triebold's Live-in Shop

14

"A lot of my parts are bar napkin sketches as well—that is the truth. You carry that over to your construction," Triebold continued. "You hate to screw with something that works. It works for me. That's when I'm the smartest, I guess."

The building was going up in 1997, and Triebold's business, Crossroads Performance, had outgrown its 1,200-square-foot rental space. He decided to build a new shop in Somerset, and put up a 4,200-square-foot steel building. At the same time this was happening, his marriage went south, and Triebold needed a space to sleep.

"I was living with a futon in the shop and a dorm fridge," he said.

This prompted him to add a living space above his new shop.

"I had some friends that would come by and would help bang something together," he said. "There were a lot of late nights."

The living space came together in about three months' time, all laid out using the bar napkin method. As he needed new spaces, he would simply add them to whichever bit of open space was available. Thanks to Triebold's natural sense of space, his efforts resulted in an attractive place with unique touches.

The living space upstairs is comfortable and has a distinct style. It not only gave Triebold a place to sleep that is better than a futon next to a work bench, but the space has become a source of pride.

Part of the place's charm comes from the salvaged materials. Triebold scrounged doors and windows from local construction salvage stores. Bits like the tall solid wood doors and windows came from old schools.

Above left: The sheetmetal interior walls are stylish and also bounce light throughout the inside of the building. **Above right:** These interior doors came from a school. Triebold chose them because they allow plenty of natural light to filter through the building. **Below:** A homebuilt table makes working on the motorcycle less of a back strain. Building such a thing would take even a semi-competent carpenter half a day.

"Some of the stuff came out of an old science lab," Triebold said. "I had a buddy that was remodeling a school and he would bring things over that he thought would be cool."

One of the challenges Triebold faced was getting light into the space. He was attracted to school doors because they have large window panels on them, which helped him bounce light across the structure.

"Bouncing the light is very important," Triebold said. "That is something that is so subtle that it goes unnoticed. You have to take special care and consideration to bounce the light. Natural light is being bounced from the south side to the north side of the building. Anyplace you can put glass in helps. I was looking for a big open glass kind of door, so that's how I happened going after the salvage stuff.

"The big doors—the entrance doors—are from an old school from the 1920s. It makes the space unique."

Triebold also used tin walls, silver paint, interior windows, and angled panels to direct light into the middle of the space. The result is that the space feels bright despite a large portion of the walls having no exterior exposure.

"That lunch room kind of built itself. It was leftover space. It's a great space. There are no windows in

Right: Crossroads Performance is a machine shop specializing in motorcycle speed parts, and the home of the owner, Mark Triebold. The interior layout uses walls laced with windows to allow natural light into the building and give it a more open feel. **Below:** Signatures on the wall honor all the friends and family who helped Mark build his dream garage.

it. The shades that are in it are just shades—there is nothing behind them. You create the illusion of windows with the shades."

Triebold's need for space came as his business expanded. He founded the business in the early 1990s, after about a decade as a machinist, working with metal, and then moving to management and more administrative work. He decided to start Crossroads Performance to build performance parts. His first product line was oriented around the Harley-Davidson Sportster.

The fact that the Sportsters handle better than other Harley-Davidsons is attractive to Triebold. He also likes the fact that they offer solid performance for a price that is considerably lower than other Harleys.

"Sportsters offer the cheapest bang for the buck horsepower-wise," Triebold said.

The aftermarket parts sold well enough to keep the doors open, and the line soon included parts for Buell motorcycles. In the mid-1990s, Triebold made a deal with Buell to set them up with a complete line of performance parts. That deal led to the construction of Triebold's new shop, as his company couldn't build the Buell parts line in a 1,200-square-foot space.

"We helped them get that whole Pro Series line of parts together," Triebold said. "We received some attractive orders from that. That was our big break."

One of the pleasures of putting that together was working with Erik Buell, the engineer and former racer who created the Buell Motorcycle Company.

"He was pretty absorbed with making his company work when I first met him. He'd spend most of his time walking around frantically rubbing his head," Triebold said. "If you could get him away from work, he's a great guy to hang out with. He's into old Studebakers and liked to play guitars—we had a lot in common."

Crossroads Performance grew beyond just the Buell account, and they now have a client list that includes Drag Specialties, Clockwerx, and Kuryakyn. Thanks to his living space being built into the shop, Triebold was right there on the grounds to make sure the business ran smoothly. .

"It's a pretty fast-paced business," Triebold said. "It's extremely convenient to be so close by. I can go out there and bark orders at the guys in my pajamas."

While that convenience led to business success, it also became a bit of a burden. In 2006, Triebold bought an 80-acre farm that he escapes to on weekends.

"My roots are very rural," Triebold said. "Living in town kind of drove me nuts. I need room for tractors and things like that. Plus, it keeps me humble. It's hard to get too big of a head when you are picking rock and baling hay."

He also had completed the work on his shop in Somerset and was ready for a new project. So he's building his dream hobby farm one building at a time.

And drawing them on cocktail napkins, of course.

Facing page: Ol' Blue is a custom Sportster built by Triebold. The 1200cc nitrous-injected engine uses Buell Thunderstorm heads and a Vance & Hines SS2R exhaust. The chassis is sprung with Buell 54mm inverted forks and Progressive shocks. **Below:** Triebold lives above the shop and keeps his workout equipment below.

Left: This working shop is a testament to building a space practically and economically. The trim is simply pine, and the wall is covered in sheet metal. Looks great, costs next to nothing. **Above:** Mark's living space is inside the shop. This bar is downstairs, with bedrooms in the loft above. The living room above uses exposed rafters covered in sheet metal to give it a distinct look. **Below:** The break room was one of the last to be built, mainly due to the fact that it was the last needed space.

HAVE YOU HAD YOUR
SPANKING TODAY?

THE ONLY MARK
YOU'LL MAKE IN LIFE
IS ON YOUR SHORTS!

I WOKE THIS MORNING
STICKY, BROKE & CONFUSED!

DRUG TESTING
Pisses Me Off!

ALL I WANT IS
IS A LITTLE MORE
THAN I'LL EVER GET!

POW-MIA
YOU ARE NOT FORGOTTEN

I DON'T DRIVE FAST,
JUST FLY LOW!

AVE YOU HAD YOUR
SPANKING TODAY?

STREET ROD

BALLOON

1914 Excelsior

DO NOT Touch Please!

If you happen to have any kind of motorcycling bent, the Garage Company will have things you want. The motorcycles run the gamut from exotic race bikes such as a 1991 Ducati 851 to wild customs such as a 1914 Excelsior customized by famed builder Shinya Kimura. In the unlikely case that a motorcycle on the floor doesn't quite suit your tastes, maybe you'll lust after a 1990s back issue of *Cycle World*, a vintage motocross jersey, or a Rat Fink scale model.

If not, keep looking. The place is so packed you can barely navigate the aisles. Vintage gas pumps mingle with Ascot TT posters, Bultaco and Budweiser signs, and Harley KR motors.

Yoshi's Vintage *Valhalla* 15
The Garage Company

The helmet collection alone is so extraordinary that a French magazine did a feature article on it.

So finding a bit of moto-lust that suits you is unlikely to be a problem. The question is whether your bauble of choice is for sale.

The owner of the store, Yoshinobu "Yoshi" Kosaka, is a fixture in southern California motorcycle circles. His shop came about simply because Yoshi loves bikes and his wife, Kyoku, got tired of their home being cluttered up with dozens of motorcycles and parts.

Yoshi came to America from Japan in the 1980s. He brought a few bikes with him, and added to his collection by spending his life perusing swap meets, garage sales, and classified ads. Later-model vintage

bikes and parts were cheap back then, and he picked up a lot of them for next to nothing. When his collection exceeded 100 bikes and countless parts, Kyoku took action.

She rented him a storefront in Venice Beach in the 1980s, and Yoshi and his stuff promptly started spending all of their free time at the garage. People wandered in thinking it was a motorcycle shop, and the couple decided to print some T-shirts to sell to the wannabe customers. The shirts sold like hotcakes, and the couple decided to rent a 5,400-square-foot space on Washington Boulevard and make a business out of it. The Garage Company was born.

While Yoshi now runs the shop as a business, selling and building motorcycles and parts, much of

Above left: The Garage Company has a little bit of everything, ranging from motorcycles for sale to books, magazines, and model kits. Bikes for sale at the shop in February 2009 included a Rickman-framed Z1 Kawasaki racer ($20,000), a Von Dutch customized supercharged 1947 Indian (make offer), and a 1991 Ducati 851 race bike ($21,500; price includes shipping from Japan). **Below:** This Excelsior custom was built by Shinya Kimura, who founded well-known Japanese customization shop Zero Engineering in 1992 and moved on to create Chabott Engineering in 2006. Shinya's bikes created the "Zero Style" look, a minimalist style that drew motorcycle fans of all stripes to customs.

the stuff you'll find in the storefront are his personal goodies. The Shinya-built Excelsior, for example. And the collection of vintage gauges.

Not for sale.

The Garage Company has branched out in recent years and is building custom motorcycles. The machines tip their hats to 1950s customizers, and are mostly bobbers with lots of options available for the customer. Original parts meld with parts found in the extensive yard at the Garage Company. The bikes are finished with Von Dutch–esque bends and tweaks to create rockabilly motorcycles sold at Kmart prices.

While Yoshi is a customizer of note himself, he also has several gifted resident mechanics. Both restorer Joe Yee and builder Takashi Iwamoto are starting to make names for themselves with the machines they have created.

The shop built a bike for retired Formula 1 racer Michael Schumacher in 2006, and Yoshi's customer list includes rock star Brian Setzer and tattoo artist and Von Dutch devotee Ed Hardy.

Yoshi had vintage raced in Japan and kept up his hobby when he came to America. He even collected a title in 1993, winning the Formula 250 class on a Bultaco. His collection of motorcycles reflects his racing ways. You'll find a couple of Honda factory racers, an MV Augusta 350 four-cylinder, and a Harley KR-TT, among many others.

More than a decade ago, he called up the organizers of vintage racing in California and landed himself the job of promoting a race. Now his shop annually sponsors the Corsa MotoClassica at Willow Springs. The weekend includes vintage racing, a swap meet, and plenty of bench racing the last week in April.

A stop down to The Garage Company is a mandatory part of any gearhead's visit to Los Angeles. Just be prepared—your checkbook may not be enough to bring home your toy of choice.

Left: Yoshi Kosaka (behind the counter) is the owner of Garage Company, an eclectic vintage motorcycle and customization shop in Los Angeles. Yoshi's customization work is outstanding, and he is also the man behind the Corsa MotoClassica, an annual weekend of vintage racing and more held at Willow Springs Raceway. **Following spread:** Four original choppers were used in the classic film *Easy Rider*. Three were stolen, and one was destroyed and later rebuilt and sold at auction in 2001. This one built at the Garage Company is a replica of *Captain America*, the bike ridden by Peter Fonda in the film. The frame is an original surviving piece from one of the bikes used in the film, discovered by Yoshi.

Above: This beautifully crafted tank rests near the award-winning Harley racer in the shop. **Right:** Powerplant Choppers are built by Yaniv Evan in a shop not far from the Garage Company. The expensive machines look great. **Below:** You can spend hours in the Garage Company, perusing books, magazines, and the long list of goodies stashed in cases.

Above left: More interesting bits can be found in this crate in the back of the shop. **Above right:** The back lot at the Garage Company is full of interesting machines like this Evel Knievel–inspired custom built by the shop. **Below:** Most of these bits are not for sale.

Racer's Refuge

As the bars on Daytona's beer-soaked Main Street chased out their last customers in mid-October of 2001, Chris Cosentino was frantically trying to get his bike together. Pulling an all-nighter to prep a racing motorcycle for an outing on Daytona's banked oval is a bit of a tradition among long-time racers, but it was a first for Cosentino. He had done plenty of racing with Honda RS125s and had not needed to go these lengths just to make a race.

The CCS races at Daytona in October 2001 were special because the bike Cosentino was preparing was of his own design. He had built the machine in the spring and was now determined to test the bike's mettle on the track.

Street of Dreams

Chris Cosentino's New Jersey Shop

16

The machine used an innovative front suspension system and was stuffed with a Rotax single-cylinder engine. The result was very light, powerful, and agile. The bike was complete and running, but it was raw and utterly untested.

"The frame was still warm from welding as we were loading it into the trailer," he said. "It really wasn't quite ready yet, but ... I was going to take that bike and race it."

After a very long and troublesome weekend trying to get it tuned properly, he managed to make his race and came in second to last in Heavyweight Sportsman. Just getting the bike running and limping it through the race was a victory of sorts, but Cosentino learned some hard lessons at Daytona.

The first was that building a race bike of your own design was possible, as he believed. Sorting that machine out and turning it into a functioning machine was a much more difficult challenge that he hadn't anticipated.

His expectations going into the weekend were very high. An engineer and lifetime tinkerer and builder, Cosentino believed that if he assembled a package that worked on paper, he would triumph at the track. He was right, but it wasn't as simple as he imagined.

He said he thought, "'If I build a bike that weighs this much and makes this much power, I should be able to beat all these other people.' On paper you can do that—but once you get in the real world there are a lot more details that have to be taken care of."

Above left: Cosentino's day job is designing prototype parts for clients. His shop is outfitted with CNC mills, lathes, tubing benders, a welding room, and polishers and grinders. He can design and build almost any part. **Above right:** CAD drawings remain a key component to building the race bike. **Below left:** Cosentino's shop has the dual function of hosting his fabrication business as well as his motorcycle-building hobby. Creating this motorcycle is an obsession that has absorbed all of his spare resources. He puts in long hours at this shop, doing everything from ignition curve tuning to designing the engine's custom-built crank and rods.

Once those details were sorted, Cosentino's hand-built race bike became a front-runner in CCS's lightweight classes. In fact, the team had to run in the ASRA Thunderbike class to find serious competition.

Cosentino started down the path of turning CAD drawings into hand-built racing motorcycles by hanging out at his father's little two-bay service station. He built a kart from scratch, then moved on to dirt bikes, riding in the forests near his home.

By the time he was in high school, his interests turned to cars. When he left to study engineering at The Cooper Union in Manhattan, he was driving a modified 1968 Camaro.

"It was a total hot rod that was not appropriate for Manhattan. You know, a stick shift, a stiff clutch, no power steering." Chris said. "The thing fucking rocked but it was definitely not a city driver."

He sold the Camaro and moved on to motorcycles, which were a better fit for a college student's budget and space constraints. The Cooper Union is an art, engineering, and architectural school that emphasizes teaching talented students how to make positive contributions to society. The results-oriented environment turned out to be a good fit for Cosentino. He dutifully absorbed engineering theory, and his aptitude for building things with his hands made him the lab partner of choice in his class.

His mechanical skills came into play with his first streetbike, a powerful but notoriously poor-handling Kawasaki KZ1000. Not long after he bought it, he crashed hard. The machine was nearly a total loss. He tore the bike down and completely modified it with a new fork and custom-built swingarm. His hand-built additions improved the Kawasaki's performance and his self-assurance.

"I had the confidence from having done all this shit as a kid," he said. "You realize that you can build something, and, yeah, I'll go ride it and if I break my ass, I break my ass. If I don't, I don't."

He moved up to a Yamaha R1 and met fellow hardcores Todd Puckett and Gregor Halenda shortly thereafter. They spent their weekends riding on Bear Mountain. They liked to ride hard, and soon decided the track was a safer place to do that. After a couple of track days got them hooked, they gave vintage racing a go, thinking it was a cheap way to get into the sport.

Chris Cosentino with the race bike he designed and built at his shop in New Jersey. The frame was custom-built and CAD-designed, while the Frankenstein of an engine is a Rotax single bottom end fabricated to work with a Ducati 1098 top end.

They soon discovered that vintage racing is hardly cheap, and moved to racing Honda RS125s. These light racers are incredibly fun to ride and are favored by experienced racers. They weigh in at about 150 pounds, less than half the weight of nearly any other motorcycle you'll see at the track.

"So it's almost like being a hummingbird," Chris said. "It felt like riding a little razor blade."

That whet his appetite for light racing motorcycles. He also wanted more of a challenge than just racing a production bike.

"I believed there had to be a better way," Cosentino said, "and I could find a better way because I'm a smart guy."

As he looked deeper into how racing rules are structured, he saw that the only classes that would allow him to race his hand-built bikes were for single-cylinder machines. So he put some time in designing a very light, single-cylinder race bike.

Cosentino's training is in CAD, so he started sketching a chassis on the computer. CAD allows a lot of experimentation without requiring the designer to build test parts out of metal. After a couple of years of tinkering, Cosentino had a sophisticated, innovative chassis design.

Designing in CAD is so efficient, it can eventually become a limitation. "Some people just keep clicking on the computer," Cosentino said, "and some people walk into the shop and start building. So I walked into the shop and started building."

His first prototype used an air-cooled Rotax single-cylinder engine—the design he debuted at Daytona in 2001. Making that motorcycle competitive required hundreds of hours of labor.

Once that was sorted out, the bike was reasonably fast and very strong in its class. More power was required to move up a class, and the Rotax air-cooled single could only stretch so far.

This Norton engine serves as high-performance art in Chris' shop.

When a friend bought a scrapped Ducati 999 engine from eBay, a light went off in Cosentino's head. The Duc's top end could provide the additional horsepower he wanted.

So he went to work designing all the parts necessary to graft the desmoquattro top end to the Rotax bottom end. To make that work, Cosentino hand-fabricated so many parts that the engine is essentially a custom design.

He put the chassis through a second design evolution, and the result is an integrated piece. The engine is designed for the chassis, and vice versa.

The Cosentino custom is impressive on the track, running wheel to wheel with larger-displacement twin-cylinder machines such as highly modified Buell 1200s and Suzuki SV650s. The engine has been upgraded from a 999 to Ducati's newer 1098 top end, with stellar horsepower output and dicey reliability.

As practical as he is analytical, Cosentino realized a few years ago that his riding skills were becoming the bike's limiting factor. To stay at the front, he recruited his friend Todd Puckett to take the controls.

Cosentino has already gone from images on a screen to a class-dominating race bike. Yet he believes there's even more speed and prowess in his design, which a third generation can bring to perfection. At that point he could produce the bike commercially.

He has much of his life invested in this machine, both personally and financially. He has single-handedly designed and built a bike that can beat offerings from multi-million-dollar corporations. But Cosentino can't make the refinements necessary for commercial success on his own. He has to find an investor who is equally committed to winning races on two wheels.

Raising money is never easy, and that is doubly true in 2009. Even given a chilly investment climate,

Cosentino at speed on his race bike. Cosentino modified the engine to use a Ducati desmoquattro top end on a Rotax bottom. The bike became fast enough to compete against motorcycles with nearly double the displacement. *Cosentino Collection*

he was able to secure an investor interested in using the chassis in the FIM's Grand Prix series. The rules for the 250 class have changed for 2010, with four-stroke engines being used in the new class to be called "Moto2." Cosentino is preparing a bike to run a few races in 2009 and a full season in 2010.

So the life Cosentino has built continues. The long night working at Daytona was not the first spent on the bike, nor will it be his last.

The shop is a second home to him, and he spends plenty of late nights drawing parts and dyno testing, mining imagination's ores, and forging them into a racing motorcycle built to conquer reality's cold black tarmac.

Facing page: Data acquisition is a key component to any race bike. Cosentino uses a Mychron2-gold system on the bike.
Above: Cosentino grew up tinkering with lawn mowers, bicycles, and whatever else he found at his father's gas station. He built his own kart. "It really just started off with me being a total gearhead at my dad's station," Chris said. *Cosentino Collection*
Below: The FIM's new class, Moto2, will replace the two-stroke powered 250 class. Bikes in Moto2 will run four-stroke engines.

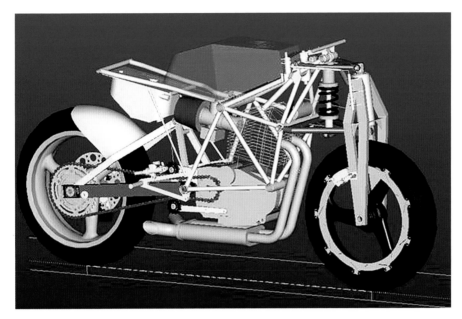

Left: The race bike started from Chris doodling on the computer, a process that is not atypical for engineers. His drawing got more and more sophisticated. Where Chris departed from the usual was that he actually built the bike he designed. *Chris Cosentino*
Below: Cosentino will be using his chassis in an entry in the new Moto2 class debuting FIM racing in 2010. This is an early CAD drawing of the bike. *Chris Cosentino* **Facing page:** The race bike is a second-generation design. The first-gen frame has found a home in some extra space in the shop. "We have taken the second-generation bike to the limit," Chris said. "We need a third-generation bike to take the next step, and it's going to take a chunk of change to do that. There's no sense in going further unless we can make this into a business."

Speed comes in all kinds of packages. Lion-hearted racers like Dick Mann hardheadedly smash racetracks into submission. Supremely talented James Stewart and Kenny Roberts mix confidence, fearlessness, and innate ability into a ballsy throttle-twisting cocktail that destroys the competition.

Speed also comes to the precise, those to whom a set of handlebars is a scalpel and a wheel a blade. These racers slice and dice racetracks with an engineer's precision, finding the fastest way around the circuit with minimal touches to the machine.

The Artisan of Speed 17
John Hateley

I was barely old enough to pedal a bicycle when John Hateley was kicking mud into the competition's faces, and therefore I have no idea what kind of racer he was in top form. I can tell you, however, that watching him knife a pristinely prepared flat tracker around the little track at his idiosyncratic dream garage with a foot out and canted in just so makes me think I know. He's got National-Level Championship Speed, by the way. Not the garden-variety shit you see down at your favorite track doing heel-clickers and whips and making the local boys gawk. He's the Real Deal and was the first racer in history to earn both motocross and flat track AMA national numbers.

The thing that makes me suspect Hateley's talents tend toward the scalpel rather than the hammer happened after he got off the bike and parked it on the slab of concrete in front of his converted Model A garage. As the bike sat ticking and cooling, Hateley came out of his garage with a leaf blower to carefully clean the dust off the bike and the concrete pad.

The style on the track and the attention to detail leads me to believe that Hateley's speed is the razor's edge of precision, the type where you know the man will hit the same line lap after lap after lap.

Hateley's nose for precision carries into the meticulous madness you'll find inside the gearhead candy store that he calls a garage at his place in California's Santa Clarita Valley. Every nook and cranny is jammed with storied race bikes, hand-fabricate enticements, and pieces of moto-history.

And his mind is as organized as his shop when it comes to telling the stories behind each motorcycle tidbit. He can tell about the Triumph chopper that was used on the set of the movie *Bubble Boy* or the

Above left: John at speed on an XT500-based flat tracker that he and a friend built and are considering offering for sale commercially. The bikes are cheap and effective race machines. **Above right:** Hateley is meticulous with his tools and his garage. **Below left:** Former racer, Hollywood stunt man, and bike builder John Hateley calls this old Model A garage in southern California home. He bought it in the 1980s, and turned an overgrown junkyard into a gearhead's dream.

500 Cheney-framed Triumph twin his father, Jack, had built for motocross racing. Or the sign on the wall reading 98 miles per hour that was set up as a speed limit sign for a deathly set of whoops he used to ride.

In fact, Hateley warned me to be careful.

"Every one of these things has a story," he said. "Don't ask me about anything unless you want to listen." I focused on the bits that pertained to John's professional racing or Hollywood stunt man career—mostly.

But the tractor seat on the CR80 was just too much.

"John," I said. "What is *this*?"

He explained that his sons had gotten into building motorcycles at a young age, when both boys were under 10 years old. The kids started assembling the motorcycle out of bits lying around the place.

"It was harmless," Hateley said, "until I heard Keenan tell Ajay, 'No, it'll be fine, go ahead and go for it.'" The boys were on top of a 100-foot-high embankment on the property, and the older one had the six-year-old set down on the tractor seat. He was planning to push his younger brother down the hill, shod in safety gear that consisted of tennis shoes and a ball cap. That was the end of the Frankenstein bike project.

Hateley's converted garage is full of the makings of more Frankenstein creations, and it houses more history than a county museum. The structure started life as a rec room built for an eccentric land baron and later became a Model A garage. Hateley and his wife, Candace, bought the place in the 1980s.

The junk was neck-deep, and Hateley spent several years cleaning out barrels of exhaust pipe, an old incinerator, and literally tons of rusting parts. As the crap came out, the Hateley collection of bikes, memorabilia, and tools were moved in.

Hateley's love affair with motorcycles began with his father, Jack Hateley. Jack and a partner started Triumph of Burbank in the mid-1960s. As John grew into his teens, his talents as a racer grew and his father tuned motorcycles for him as well as for another pro racer.

John was racing professionally by the time he was 15 years old and went on to win national championships in AMA Dirt Track and Motocross

The inside of the garage houses a mix of machines that would make any motorcycle lover mad. Many of the bikes are flat track racers, and the hot rods both were used or built by John's father, Jack.

arenas, was a consistent top competitor at national speedway events, and made competitive runs in the Baja 1000.

One of the pieces of history at rest in Hateley's garage in the Santa Clarita Valley is a Triumph flat tracker. Hateley's father, Jack, was adamant that they promote their brand when John was out racing, which meant that some very special motorcycles were built.

One of these was created in 1965, when Jack had a Triumph twin shoehorned into a BSA Goldstar chassis. As the bike was being built, Jack decided to have local painter and customizer Kenny Howard tool the shop's name into the oil tank. Better known as "Von Dutch," the creative customizer and gearhead had become a phenomenon by the time he did the

tank for Jack. But Jack had known Von Dutch for years, and he was a local painter-personality as far as he was concerned.

Young Hateley was assigned with the task of taking the tank to Von Dutch and later picking up the completed part. When he came back with the piece, it had been done in true Von Dutch style, with wild designs and intricate tooling.

"The thing looked like a piece of graffiti," Hateley said. "My dad went nuts!"

Jack so disliked the art he welded a plate on the side to form a scoop on the oil tank to cover it up. With a flashlight, you can shine light behind the scoop and see the Von Dutch metal work, which is now probably the most valuable part of the motorcycle.

Jack Hateley owned Triumph of Burbank, and John grew up surrounded by motorcycles. He started racing at a young age and watched legendary racers like Eddie Mulder and Dusty Coppage come into the shop on a regular basis.

Above left: The walls of the Hateley shop are lined with interesting tidbits. **Below:** Flat track racing is one of the cornerstones of Hateley's career. His father, Jack, didn't care to compete in flat track, but his shop was a center for the sport in the 1960s and 1970s. And John didn't share his dad's fear of the wall.

Hateley's father's influence is prevalent in the vehicles that cover the garage. A blue Cheney-framed Triumph 500 is one of those. As motocross became prevalent in America in the mid-1960s, the Hateleys decided to give the new sport a shot. Despite the fact that Triumph of Burbank sold Greeves and CZ—two makes that built some of the most competitive motocross bikes of the time—Jack insisted that his son go to the track on a Triumph.

Cheney was a small company in Britain that made motocross frames for Triumph twins, and Jack built his son a race bike using one of them. John competed in the first District 37 motocross race in California on the Cheney. He won, beating riders on lighter and more agile two-stroke bikes. He later won the 500 expert class at the Hopetown Grand Prix on the bike. The bike became a bit of a legend from that win.

In 1975, John Hateley spent a year riding for the Triumph-Norton factory team in the AMA Nationals. The short-track 350cc bike he rode was built by his father's apprentice, Steve Storz. Storz went on to found Storz Performance, which is now one of the best-known builders of Harley-Davidson and Buell performance equipment. He still has that bike, and it is one of three that remain.

As Hateley's professional racing career wound down, he began his second career as a Hollywood stunt man. He rode motorcycles in dozens of major motion pictures, including performing stunts and supplying motorcycles to more than 50 feature films, including *The Italian Job, The Crow, Speed,* and *Wayne's World*.

One of his best-known scenes was wheelying a military bike while chasing a sidecar-equipped motorcycle during the filming of *Indiana Jones and the Last Crusade*. The director was urging Hateley to get as close as possible to the rear of the sidecar, so John wheelied the bike and dropped his front tire into the sidecar rig. Amazingly, he didn't crash while pulling off the maneuver. It didn't look quite right on film, though, so another of his wheelies that came close to the sidecar rig went into the final cut.

Hateley made several appearances in films as an actor, and also developed a reputation for building and supplying motorcycles for the movies. He also built a few bikes for people in the business, including a one-off custom with "titanium everything" for former Grand Prix rider John Kocinski.

As fond as John is of his personal race bikes and bits of Hollywood memorabilia in his garage, two hot rods are among his favorites.

A row of number 98s.

One is a car built in 1956 by an old mechanic who worked for John's dad. The car spent hundreds of Wednesday nights cruising and misbehaving on Van Nuys Boulevard. John bought the car in 1980 and restored it to period-correct condition. The rod is a bit of a time capsule. When Hateley cleaned out the doors, he found a paper trail from his dad's formative years, which included receipts from Bob's Big Boy, drag slips from San Fernando Raceway, and gas tickets from when fuel cost 37 cents per gallon.

He also has a 1929 Model A lakester that his dad raced in the 1980s. With it, his father set a world speed record for flathead four-cylinder cars of 118 miles per hour in 1983. Hateley loves the fact that these cars were hand-built, and calls them "non-UPS cars."

"There's a tradition to it," Hateley said. "He was taught to build parts using a hacksaw and a file. It wasn't dropped off at his doorstep to bolt on."

The cars hold a special mystique for Hateley, in part because they are part of a scene in life that he skipped right past.

"I missed the whole hot rod, high school thing that my dad went through," Hateley said. "I had a van like you see sitting there that held three dirt track bikes, eighty-five gallons of gas, and a little bunk. We went all over the country racin' dirt track."

So John's formative years were spent on the racetrack putting his dad's equipment through the paces. He also carried on his father's tradition and learned to build his own race bikes.

Even today, Hateley is constantly building some kind of interesting motorcycle or car. The old Model A garage is not just a museum where the past is hermetically sealed to be studied. Hateley's space is more of a living experiment, as new pieces of motorcycle lore and legend are built and then piled, tacked, or parked in this meticulous gearhead's southern California playground.

The "98 MPH" sign used to be on a set of particularly vicious whoops at one of John's favorite racetracks.

Hateley's converted garage is full of the makings of more Frankenstein creations, and it houses more history than a county museum.

Left: Hateley is one of the few racers to have won at the national level in motocross, flat track, and roadracing events. **Below:** Most of Hateley's bikes wear his AMA number 98. **Following Spread:** Hateley builds bikes for occasional customers in his shop. One of those happens to be the infamously fussy former Grand Prix racer John Kocinski.

Facing page: Hateley saved some of the parts stashed at his place when he bought it. Some of the old flathead engines are valuable pieces. **Right:** John didn't appear on *The Tonight Show*, but one of his motorcycles did. **Below:** John's Triumph flat track racer.

Acknowledgments

First off, I'd like to thank all the garage owners who took time to show me their places and tell their stories. It was an honor and a joy. Mike and Nuri Wernick were particularly helpful, supplying extra images and sort of taking me into the fold. Ditto with Peter Dietrich and Chris Cosentino at Spannerland. Geby Wager, Patti Cook, and Stefanie Giddens at Woodland Hills couldn't have been more welcoming. The B.S. session with Robert Genise and the boys at John's Cycle Center made for a great afternoon, as did a couple of hours at Hugh Mackie's Sixth Street Specials with Fumihisa Matsueda. I spent four of the most interesting hours of my life immersed in motorcycle racing lore at John Hateley's place and will never forget that. I also had great experiences with Jeff Gilbert, Tom White, Mark Triebold, Kelly Owen, and Yoshi Kosaka.

Second, I'd like to thank those who provided leads. Karel Kramer, Vinnie Mandzak, Sam Martin, Zack Miller, and particularly Rick Schunk, who knows everyone in classic bikes and graciously opened his little black book to me.

Schunk also contributed two stories to the book. Thanks to the others who contributed: Kris Palmer, Mike Seate, and Peter Martin.

Thanks to the people at Motorbooks: Nichole Schiele for her work in publicity; Jeffrey Zuehlke for shepherding the project along; and to Kris Palmer for his careful editorial work and input on the photo selection. I also owe thanks to Dennis Pernu for his helpful suggestions for the Spannerland chapter. Thanks, too, to Motorbooks publisher Zack Miller. He commissioned my first book at MBI in 1991, we worked side-by-side in the Motorbooks editorial department for 12 years, and we're still doing business nearly 20 years later. That kind of longevity doesn't happen often in today's crazy publishing world, and it's mostly because we both love motorcycles and books. Plus Zack is a good guy.

And in no particular order, thanks to Sam Wheeler for ferrying me around Seattle, to Paul Marron for directions, to Joan Hughes for being crazy enough to marry an author, and to John Koharski for all that you do.

Dedication

*To my dad,
who bought me my
first motorcycle (for $25)
even though he thought
I was crazy to ride it.*

— LK —

Index

Bikes

BMW, 124
    HP2 Enduro, 14–16
    K1200R, 17
    R1200S, 17
BSA, 57, 61, 73, 109, 124, 140, 142
    250, 57
    650cc twin, 59
    Lightning, 147
    M20, 76
Cyclone, 129, 130, 132
Douglas, 123, 127
Ducati 851, 39
Ducati, 69, 73, 123
    Desmosedici RR, 14, 16
    Mike Hailwood replica, 37
    Monster, 85
    Multistrada, 129
    SD900 Darmah, 37
Ducati-Rotax, 117, 167, 169, 171, 173
Goldmember, 26, 27
Greeves, 29, 100, 182
Harley-Davidson, 124, 129, 132, 142, 144
    883 Sportster, 121, 124
    JD, 55
    KR, 157
    KR-TT, 159
    Road King, 121
    Sport Model, 123
    Sportster, 59, 152
    VL, 39
    V-Rod, 11
    WLA, 124

Honda
    450 Nighthawk, 84
    CB750 FDNY Dream Bike, 80, 84, 87, 88, 90, 91
    CBR1000R, 14, 16
    CR110, 129
    MV Augusta, 159
    RS125, 110, 117, 118, 167, 170
    Rune, 123
    VFR, 89
Indian, 90, 124
Moto Guzzi, 69, 123, 127, 129
MTT Turbine Superbike, 11
Norton, 57, 61, 69, 73, 109, 110
    Atlas, 59
    Combat, 6
    Featherbed, 60
    single, 37
Raleigh, 121, 124, 126
Royal Enfield, 121, 124
Suzuki
    500 twin, 11
    Hayabusa, 15, 124, 126
    TM250, 33, 102
    TM400, 32
Triumph, 42, 57, 59, 61, 69, 73, 109, 110, 124, 140, 142, 179, 182, 189
    Bonneville, 57
Vincent, 41, 69, 71, 74, 109, 130
    Black Shadow, 39, 135
    Lightning, 135
Yamaha, 99
    500, 144
    R1, 169
    Seca, 84
    TT500, 99, 100
    TZ, 115

People

Aldana, David, 109, 110, 112
Allison, John, 88, 90
Baptiste, Gerard, 80, 84, 87, 88
Cosentino, Chris, 110, 114, 116, 117, 167, 169–171, 173, 175
Dye, Edison, 95, 97, 102, 105
Free, Rollie, 69, 73, 76, 135
Genise, Frankie and John, 139, 144
Genise, Robert, 139, 140, 142–144, 147
Gilbert, Jeffrey, 129, 130, 132, 134, 135
Goldammer, Roger, 7, 14, 26, 27, 71
Halenda, Gregor, 110, 114, 117, 169
Hamel, Steve, 69, 71, 73, 75, 76
Hateley, Jack, 177, 179, 180, 182, 184
Hateley, John, 177, 179–182, 184, 185, 189
Hood, George, 47, 48, 51, 54, 55
Jones, Gary, 95, 100
Juchli, Bernard, 37, 39
Juchli, Rosalie, 37, 39, 41
Kocinski, John, 182, 185

Kosaka, Yoshinobu "Yoshi," 157, 159
Leno, Jay, 11, 37, 39, 41
Mackie, Hugh, 57, 59–62, 64, 66, 107, 109, 114, 142
Matsueda, Fumihisa, 59, 64
Munro, Burt, 69, 73, 75, 76
O'Grady, Tim, 88, 90
Owen, Kelly, 29, 32, 34
Peter, 107, 109, 110, 112, 116, 117
Roberts, Kenny, 109, 177
Solomon, Barry, 121, 123
Triebold, Mark, 149, 150, 152, 155
Turin, Dimitri, 59, 61
Vogel, Chuck, 47, 51
Von Dutch, 157, 159, 180
Wager, Geby, 7, 19, 20, 21, 25
Wernick, Mike, 80, 81, 83, 84, 88–91, 107
White, Brad, 100–102
White, Tom, 95, 97–102, 104, 105